CHAKRA HEALING

THE ULTIMATE PRACTICAL GUIDE TO OPEN,
BALANCE & UNBLOCK YOUR CHAKRAS AND OPEN
YOUR THIRD EYE USING SELF-HEALING
TECHNIQUES THAT HELP YOU AWAKEN

JESSICA ADAMS

CONTENTS

Introduction v

1. What Is A Chakra And Why Is It Important? 1
2. Healing The Chakras 13
3. The Root Chakra also called Muladhara 24
4. The Sacral Chakra also called Svadhisthana 42
5. The Solar Plexus Chakra Also Called Manipura 59
6. The Heart Chakra also called Anahata 78
7. The Throat Chakra also known as Vishuddha 97
8. The Third Eye Chakra 115
9. The Crown Chakra also called Sahasrara 134
10. More tools to open and heal all your chakras 152

Afterword 159
Resources 163

INTRODUCTION

In recent times as Chakras, meditation, and Yoga have gained momentum in the western world, a lot of conflicting information has been circulated around the topic. Much of the information you will encounter might end up confusing you even more. Everyone is going by what they read and interpret. Who should you believe? How many Chakra systems are there? Are Chakras really rooted in ancient sacred wisdom? Is it religious? Has it been made up in recent years? Should you even care about the topic and learn to open up and balance your Chakras?

So many questions, such few clear answers.

Years ago, I struggled to find answers to these questions and more. So I took it upon myself to study, research and connect with practitioners and actual masters of the Sanskrit (since that's where it is said to originate) so I could get answers for myself.

This same quest has led me to share the same knowledge and healing I have received with you dear reader in the hopes that if you too have been seeking answers and solutions for leading a more holistic, connected and healthy life, you may use the strategies and knowledge contained within this book to transform your life.

The problem with most chakra teachings:

Here's the big problem when you're faced with the challenge of opening and balancing your chakras. It seems like everyone is trying to prove that their method is the right and only way. Instead of simplifying, the trend appears to be complicating it and making it seem elusive. As if that can ever help someone who is in dire need of answers.

Those that speak on the topic do nothing more than share vague ideas that seem impractical for the modern individual to fully engage in. If you've been struggling to find a simple solution, I've got good news. The search is now over.

You will now have a practical guide to the chakra system and how to balance and open up your chakras. I have been practicing spirituality for decades at this point. I've received training and certifications on Yoga Nidra, Chakra Balancing, Meditation and Stress Reduction, Crystal Healing, Angelic Healing, and I could go on and on. As you can see, any kind of training that involves healing has been a passion of mine, perhaps because, at one point, I too struggled to feel healthy, whole, and connected with life. The result of my in-depth study and devotion to these classes has enabled me to help people with meditation, yoga, and opening up and balancing their chakras, and so much more.

To date, one of my favorite classes is the one where I take my students through chakra healing, where we learn about the energy centers in the body, which are the energy vortexes that we call Chakra. These energy centers have been mapped out for at least five thousand years. In fact, many teachers believe the teachings of the chakras have been around far longer than that, albeit not in the manner which we teach in modern times. Learning to open up and balance all your chakras will aid you in reclaiming the balance within your mind and body that you've been struggling to get. It will increase your concentration levels, self-awareness, and improve your general well-being. Many of the mental and emotional issues that have weighed you down in the past will no longer form part of your daily experience. You will have an easier time detaching to things that no longer serve you. Failure to consciously work on unblocking your Chakra may cause you to continue struggling with your health, connecting with yourself and others. Most people don't realize that horrible eating habits, chronic pain, intimacy issues, financial lack are all symptoms of a blocked chakra system.

So what I want to bring to you with this book is the simplified version of how you can begin to understand, work with and align the energy systems of your body for a greater experience of life. If there are significant changes you wish to experience in your life, acquiring this book now and reading it cover to cover will prove to be one of the best investments you could ever make for yourself.

Your true nature:

If you only trusted and lived from the belief that what you see is all there is, then you'd believe that everything around us and our own bodies are unmoving or solid. Everything tends to appear static. Pretty much the same way looking out at the horizon by the beach, the world seems flat, and the sun seems to move. But the fact is the earth is round, not flat. It is always spinning and moving around the sun, not the other way around. And even though the planet looks like one giant mass, it is composed of various elements.

In the same light, what we see with our eyes and what we've been led to believe our bodies are cannot be the whole story.

We are all energy, and that energy radiates from our chakras outward. Our bodies are composed of trillions of cells, all made of particles that are always in motion. Each of these particles carry a magnetic charge that is responsible for how we interact with our world physically, emotionally, and spiritually. Just as our planet earth is composed of different types of elements, our physical body contains different types of energy. The chakra system is one that's meant to help us understand how these various energy centers within our body correspond to our physical health, relationships, finances, and more.

If you were highly attuned to reading energy or auras, you'd be able to see a colored light surrounding you. That color changes depending on whether you're happy, angry, sad, etc. The stronger the emotions you feel, the stronger the light will be. I'm sure you've had moments in your life where you could feel your energy or body was "heavy" or "light," and you might have even used these terms to describe what you were experiencing. This isn't merely a figure of speech. The state of your chakra points and how balanced they are determines the flow of energy in and out of your body.

Science finally confirms what ancient traditional wisdom has known all along.

For many beginners, there's always some lingering skepticism around the scientific validity of chakra healing. Let me help put you at ease even before we jump into the teachings.

Albert Szent-Gyorgi, a Biochemist and Nobel Prize Winner, said, "In every culture and in every medical tradition before ours, healing was accomplished by moving energy". Healing traditions from Japan, Tibet, China, India, and other countries all spoke of energy channels along which the vital life-giving energy flowed. Which makes sense, right? We have channels through which blood flows, and that's vital to the health of the body, why wouldn't we also have channels through which energy flowed?

While it may seem more like woo-woo to some, science has helped reconcile logic with feeling. Our bodies are electromagnetic in nature, and science has measured these frequencies with advanced technological machines, which have resulted in the demonstration of these energy pathways. As we get further into the book, I will be sharing specific research that was recently completed, which helped validate that life is a bio-electrical and vibrational energy phenomenon. So your health revolves around balancing energy through various means.

This book contains the steps and tactics that you can use to open, balance, and unblock your seven chakras. There are, of course, way more than seven chakras, and different systems recognize different types of energy vortexes. For the purpose of giving you a basic training that is powerful enough to get you moving in the right direction, the seven chakras that we will be focused on are more than enough. It is my intention that I can give you enough valuable information to help you increase your understanding of the chakras.

Knowing how to locate, open, and harmonize your

chakra points will definitely give you an edge in life and enable you to manifest a healthier mind and body. You will learn how to note the different chakra points in your body and balance the energy coming from them. I like to consider what I am about to share with you a treasure chest containing everything you need to know about chakras to bring about self-healing and deeper spiritual connection.

1

WHAT IS A CHAKRA AND WHY IS IT IMPORTANT?

The word Chakra also spelled Cakra in Sanskrit, when literally translated means wheel or disk. In meditation and yoga, we use this term to refer to the wheels of energy that are located throughout the body. For thousands of years, chakras have been depicted as spinning, colored wheels of energy, and have been recognized as essential to life by many ancient schools of thought, especially Hinduism and Tantric Buddhism.

They are perceived as focal points where psychic energy and bodily functions merge and interact with each other. If you can imagine any large building with running electricity, we know that there must be numerous electrical circuits and wires which meet at certain junction points where primary connections are happening. Similarly, in the human body, we are taught that there over one hundred junction points that form energy centers. And these are generally referred to as chakras. They are often visualized as circles. Still, many sages and practitioners of Sanskrit insist that the nadis always meet in the shape of a triangle. Therefore a more appropriate form for you to visualize when activating and reconnecting your chakras is a triangle.

Although here in the West we only started hearing about this subject in the early twentieth century thanks to Sir John Woodroffe, the original teachings are said to be as old or even older than 200 B.C depending on the school of thought you're ascribed to. Chakras are concentrated energy centers or vortexes within your body, and they have the responsibility of taking in, incorporating, and radiating energy to keep you functioning at optimal levels. A chakra serves as the non-physical highway through which cosmic energy travels. It connects this energy source with the physical body. Throughout this book, you'll hear me refer to this cosmic energy as Life Force or Prana. All are synonyms meant to name the same thing.

You need to understand that there are many chakras

in the body. In fact, there's still an on-going debate as to the exact number, but tantric texts name over one hundred. However, you don't need to know all the energy centers in your body to start reclaiming some balance. In fact, the core centers that you need to become aware of are only seven, and these are the ones this book is focused on.

Why do we focus on the seven chakras?

All energy workers and yogis focus on the seven chakras because the chakras correspond with massive nerve centers in the body. These are the centers that align with specific, vertically stacked key points along the midline of your physical body. They run from the base of your spine to the crown of your head. We believe the flow and alignment of the main chakras are critical to your health and vitality.

The Seven Chakras And Their Meaning

There are seven major junction points or nadis in the human body. These are referred to as the seven chakras within your body, and they exist even though you may not be able to see them. Just as you don't see your blood pumping and digestion taking place, but you know it's happening, these seven chakras are active all the time. They move the energy in and around your body through your nerve plexuses and the endocrine system.

Here's a brief breakdown of each of the seven.

The Root Chakra, also known as the Muladhara.

This Chakra is at the base of your spine. It's related to survival and security. The root chakra is the one that's closest to the earth, given that it rests at the base of your spine.

The color we associate with this Chakra is red.

The Sacral Chakra, also known as Svadhisthana.

This Chakra is in your lower abdomen. It's related to sensuality, sexuality, and pleasure. This Chakra is very much about desire.

The color we associate with this Chakra is orange.

The Solar Plexus Chakra, also known as Manipura.

This Chakra is around your navel area. It is related to power in this world. The color we associate with this Chakra is yellow.

The Heart Chakra, also known as Anahata.

This is the heart center chakra. It is related to love,

compassion, and beauty. The color associated with this Chakra is green.

The Throat Chakra, also known as Visuddha.

This Chakra is on the throat and forms your communication center. It is related to your voice, how you use it to communicate with others in your world. The color associated with this Chakra is blue.

The Third Eye chakra, also known as Ajna.

This Chakra is located between the eyebrows, and it relates to insight, awareness, intuition, and higher guidance. The color we associate with this Chakra is indigo.

The Crown Chakra, also known as Sahasrara.

This Chakra is located a little above the top of your head and represents union, bliss, and the knowledge of being at one with the Life Force. It is the silence between the space and represents spiritual connection and cosmic consciousness. The color we associate with this Chakra is violet or violet-white.

Why chakras are important:

Chakras play a vital role in our experience of life because our physical and energetic bodies are completely interconnected, and it's the chakras that are in charge of this connection. They are a direct correlation to what is going on in your physical body and life. When the chakras are open, the energy can flow freely, with positive effects for both the mind and body. But when they are closed (as is the case for most people), there's no energy flow, which creates a blockage that leads to adverse outcomes at the level of the mind and body.

Once we get this, the next logical question becomes, what is the function of the Chakra?

Glad you asked.

The primary function is to absorb the cosmic energy (Prana), metabolize it, and feed the different aspects of the human being so he or she can radiate energy outward. That is why we refer to them as energy centers. They are tasked with the responsibility of receiving and redistributing energy through the "nadis" (channels connected to the spine that have the task of transporting energy in the rest of the body). So our main intention as we go through this book is to ensure you're able to maintain the right opening and to keep things in balance once they are unblocked. We don't want any more energy blocks (closed chakras), and we certainly don't want an overload of energy (chakras too open). Whenever the chakras are either too open or closed, things get really uncomfortable for the individual.

Old Truth And New Myths To Be Aware Of

Although there's a lot of debate around what's real and what's not when it comes to chakra teachings and healing, the most important thing for you to remember is that it doesn't really matter if a teaching or technique has been modified from its original Sanskrit texts due to poor interpretation. The only thing that matters is that you find what feels right for you and what works. Some teachers will claim today's chakra teachings are false because they don't do a good enough job stating the traditional meaning from the sacred texts. Others will argue a modification is necessary to make these teachings relevant to a diverse and more modern culture. Regardless of personal sentiments, we know for a fact that chakra healing is possible, and that's all that matters. With that said, here are a few things you need to be aware of as you embark on this spiritual quest.

There are many chakra systems in your body.

The original traditional texts speak of many systems.

However, in the West, we focus on one system with the seven chakras. The theory of the subtle body and its energy centers called cakras (padmas) comes from the tradition of Tantric Yoga. This was around 600-1300 CE. In mature Tantric Yoga after the year 900, each of the many branches of the tradition articulated a different chakra system, and some branches taught more than one. Some did Five-chakra systems, six, seven, nine, ten, twelve, twenty-one, and more chakra systems are taught depending on the text and lineage you are looking at. In the Western world, we know the seven-chakra system.

So which system is right?

Well, chakras aren't like the organs in your physical body. They are not "fixed facts" that we can study like doctors study the heart. We are dealing with the energy body (sūkshma-sharīra), which is an extraordinarily fluid reality. The energy body is not static. It can present any number of energy centers depending on the person and the yogic practice he or she is performing. Having said that, however, three centers are found in all systems. These are the sexual center, the heart center, and near the crown of the head. Apart from these three, there's a huge variety in the chakra systems found in the original literature.

One is not more right than another. It all depends on your specific practice, beliefs, and the doctrine you learn.

The seven-chakra system popularized today is derived from a treatise written in 1577.

Pūrnānanda Yati wrote a Sanskrit test called "Explanation of the Six Chakras or Sat -chakra-nirūpana" in the year 1577 and it was translated into English about 100 years ago in 1918 by John Woodroffe.

The primary purpose of a chakra system is to function as a template for nyāsa.

Nyāsa means the installation of mantras and deity-energies at specific points of the subtle body. This is what the original authors were concerned with when it came to any chakra system. So even though people are so fascinated with chakra opening and balancing, very few actually use them for the intended purpose. Much of this is due to the education or lack thereof that we've received in the Western world. According to Sanskrit scholars and practitioners, the most outstanding features of the chakra systems in the original sources are the following:

1. The mystical sounds of the Sanskrit alphabet are distributed across the "petals" of all the chakras in the system.
2. That each Chakra is associated with a specific Great Element, i.e., Earth, Water, Fire, Wind, and Space.
3. That each Chakra is associated with a specific deity or deities. This is because, of course, the chakra system was primarily a template for nyāsa. How did it work? You visualize a specific mantric syllable in a specific location in a specific chakra in your energy body while silently intoning its sound.

From this, we can observe that it was culturally specific, and for the most part, this particular approach would only be beneficial to someone who grew up in that particular culture with said deities. It would only have meaning to a person who understood and believed in the meaning the practice presented.

The last point to become aware of is that the seed

mantras are meant to be for the elements, not the chakras, as is often taught.

This can be confusing, so let me do my best to simplify based on my growing understanding. Many of the teachers on the Internet will associate a certain seed-mantra (bīja) with a specific chakra. However, when we refer to any Sanskrit source, including the one written by Pūrnānanda, we don't find this connection at all. The fundamental mantras associated with the first five chakras as we know them do not belong to those chakras per se. Instead, they belong to the five Elements installed in them. You can use each of the seed mantras to install the corresponding elements in any chakra you like. For example, you can install LAM, which is the Earth element mantra, into your heart Chakra to ground your relationships. Think about how much better your relationships would be?

Benefits Of Chakra Healing

There are many benefits that you will get to enjoy once you open up, balance, and unblock your chakras. Here are just a few.

- You will feel more deeply grounded and safe

in the world and at the same time, connected to your higher self.
- It will improve your overall health and well-being.
- You'll gain a deeper understanding of your inner world and the connection between your physical and non-physical energy body.
- It will instill joy and love back into your life.
- You'll gain access to financial wisdom.
- It will allow you to express and release emotions in a healthy way.
- You will effortlessly remove any bad energy that is stored in your body.
- There will be an increased sense of self-confidence, higher self-esteem, and intuitive guidance.
- You'll feel more comfortable setting healthy boundaries that promote your well-being.
- It will help increase your mental focus concentration and memory.
- You will learn to heal yourself faster and transform weaknesses into strength.

2

HEALING THE CHAKRAS

Chakras are not only connected to particular parts of your physical body, but they also represent aspects of your consciousness. All your senses, perceptions, and possible states of awareness can be divided into seven main categories, each of which can be associated with a particular chakra. In moments where you experience tension in your consciousness, you feel it in the Chakra associated with the aspect of your consciousness experiencing the stress as well as in the parts of the physical and energy body associated with that Chakra. Therefore, it's always a good idea to self-reflect when under stress and ask yourself why you feel the stress. All tension begins at the level of consciousness before it becomes a physical manifestation. In the same way, when you feel thirsty you are already dehydrated, the physical symptoms that come about as a result of an imbalance only project a long-standing energy body imbalance.

To reverse the physical effects, we must combine both physical change and inner chakra healing practices. Remember, your natural state is that of health and homeostasis, so all we are doing in this book is getting you back into your natural state of being.

Opening and closing chakras:

We always want our chakras to be in a constant state of flow. Your body knows how to achieve this state of flow rhythmically, but often we unintentionally hinder the flow. Due to the fact that the opening and closing works like an energetic defense system, if we allow in a negative experience with its low-frequency energy to penetrate our energetic body, the corresponding Chakra can close to block that energy out. Similarly, if we get conditioned into prolonged emotional states like blame or resentment, we also close off the associated Chakra. In either scenario, special healing techniques are required to unblock the chakras. One key thing to remember as you go through this journey of life and interact with various emotions is that negative emotions carry lower energetic frequencies. These lower frequencies will almost always trigger a chakra energy constriction if not released quickly enough.

The solution isn't to isolate yourself from life and avoid all conflict and stress. Instead, it is better to equip yourself with the right tools, techniques, and education as you are doing by reading this book so that you can learn to cleanse and open your chakras as needed. As you learn to open your chakras, energy will naturally flow freely, and things will return to normal. Depending on the particular situation you're faced with, you might need to move energy throughout your body or tackle and extract a painful thorn that's stressing you out, or sometimes it might be a matter of moving yourself from a lower to a higher frequency on that emotional scale. Throughout this book, you will discover ways of being able to handle any and all of those situations.

Balance is the best solution:

Your body is always seeking to achieve energetic balance in your chakras, so we want to make sure they are neither underactive nor overactive. All seven chakras are equally essential, so just because you may feel the need to work on a specific chakra at this point in your life doesn't mean you should only work on that one to the exclusion of the others. If, for example, you've just encountered an emotionally devastating relationship, working on the heart chakra alone and getting "more energy" to flow into the heart chakra is not advisable. If one of your chakras is underactive or overactive, there's a very good chance that other chakras will fall out of alignment, creating further adverse effects on your body. This becomes very counterproductive to the energy body and chakra healing process. An underactive chakra kicks another chakra into overdrive, which in turn pulls extra energy away from that part of the body.

Before we can begin the healing practices and in-depth study of the chakras, let's go over some of the symptoms you need to become aware of so you can better judge if your chakras have been knocked out of balance.

Signs That Your Chakras Are Out Of Balance

- Restlessness, inability to sit still.
- Constipation, cramps, unhealthy weight in the form of obesity or eating disorder.
- Constant fatigue or sluggishness.

- Infertility or impotence.
- Kidney pain or infection.
- Urinary issues.
- Lower back pain or stiffness.
- Digestive problems, such as nausea, gas, ulcers, etc.
- Respiratory ailments, such as asthma.
- Nerve pain or fibromyalgia.
- Heart circulatory problems such as heart palpitations, heart attack, high blood pressure.
- Breast cancer.
- Stiff joints and joint issues in the hand.
- Sore throat.
- Dental issues.
- Earaches or infections.
- Thyroid issues.
- Stiffness or soreness in the neck or shoulders.
- Headaches and migraines.
- Insomnia or other sleep disorders.
- Seizures.
- Nightmares.
- Vision problems.

Aside from these physical symptoms, there are also

psychological effects and behavioral changes that you might want to self-asses. These are indicators that you are not feeling and acting from a place of balance and optimum health. I will break each of the chakras down with their corresponding patterns when they become either overactive or underactive.

If your root chakra is out of balance, here are some of the effects you might experience.

For an overactive root chakra, you will be fearful, struggle a lot with insecurities, and become very resistant to change. In some people, it will show up as greed or being too materialistic.

For an underactive root chakra, you will be fearful of abandonment, co-dependent, and you'll struggle with a sense of belonging. It will be hard for you to feel safe and secure or at home regardless of where you go. You might also struggle to connect with your own body.

If your Sacral Chakra is out of balance, here are some of the effects you might experience.

For an overactive sacral chakra, you will be moody, overly emotional, and attracted to drama. It's going to be hard setting healthy boundaries for yourself.

You might also find you're quick to attach to things and people.

For an underactive Sacral chakra, you will be closed off and unable to connect emotionally with yourself and others. You will feel stiff, physically, and emotionally constricted. Your self-esteem, self-worth, and self-confidence will be very low, and it will be easy to find yourself trapped in unhealthy (sometimes abusive) relationships.

If your solar plexus (naval) chakra is out of balance, here are some of the effects you might experience.

For an overactive naval chakra, you will be overly critical of yourself and others, a perfectionist in all you do. Anger, aggressiveness, and sometimes rage might be common qualities, and many will describe you as domineering.

For an underactive naval chakra, you will be indecisive, passive, and timid. It will feel as though you have no self-control.

If your heart chakra is out of balance, here are some of the effects you might experience.

For an overactive heart chakra, you will be clingy, lacking any sense of self in a relationship. You will not have any boundaries, and you might realize you're the kind of person that says yes to everything, even at the price of self-neglect. Your way of life will feel very suffocating to you.

For an underactive heart chakra, you will be grudgeful, resentful, bitter, unable, and unwilling to open up and share yourself with others. You might also be very cold and distant. This leads to a very lonely existence.

If your throat chakra is out of balance, here are some of the effects you might experience.

For an overactive throat chakra, you will find listening to be an almost impossible task. You tend to be highly critical of people, condescending, and at times, verbally abusive.

For an underactive throat Chakra, you will be introverted, shy, and unable to speak your truth and express your needs authentically. You'll have lots of difficulties to speak in public.

If your third eye chakra is out of balance, here are some of the effects you might experience.

For an overactive third eye chakra, you will be prone to hallucinations, struggle with maintaining focus and mental clarity. It will feel as though nothing you ever choose turns out right, and you'll feel out of touch with reality.

For an underactive third eye chakra, you will be disconnected and distrustful. You'll continuously self-doubt and become too reliant on external authority. You will tend to cling to the past and be fearful of the future. You'll often be closed off to new ideas and remain rigid in your thinking.

If your crown chakra is out of balance, here are some of the effects you might experience.

For an overactive crown chakra, you will have lots of difficulties controlling your emotions and easily become an addict of spirituality teachings often to the point of neglecting your bodily or material needs.

For an underactive crown chakra, you will be lacking direction and struggle with goal setting or staying focused long enough to reach them. You also won't be very open to spirituality.

Remedies For Impaired Chakras

While I will be getting into the details of each Chakra and how to bring it back to balance in the next chapter, here are some general ideas you can start implementing if you're noticing the following:

1. Something feels "off."
2. Your focus is all over the place, and you keep making silly mistakes at home or at work.
3. You keep getting sick over and over again. Like that cold, that doesn't seem to go away completely. Or you catch a cold this week, as soon as it's gone, something else starts aching.

Some powerful ways to start healing and balancing all your chakras include:

- Take frequent nature walks and spend more time out in the warmth of the sun. If there's a park nearby, a beach or a mountain, make it a priority to spend time there each week.
- Do more stretches.
- Practice breathing techniques several times a day.
- Consider taking up kundalini yoga.
- Use flower essences under your tongue or in water to bring about a positive, energetic shift. Remember, this is not to be confused

with aromatherapy oils. Flower essences possess no scent at all as they are simply the healing vibration of a blossom, preserved in brandy and water.

- Visualize and use deep breathing to cleanse your chakras. You can envision yourself cocooned in bright white light and then pour healing energy to any chakra you want to heal. Do this repeatedly and give your chakras a regular visualization healing to keep them inflow.
- Light a bundle of dried white sage similar to how we light incense then intentionally move it around your energy field. In essence, you want to give yourself a smoking sage bath. Don't forget to safely extinguish the sage by running it under water once the bath is done.
- Aromatherapy oil burner or an oil diffuser can have extremely healthy benefits for your mind, body, and chakras. Consider using the appropriate essential oil regularly to bring about healing for the desired Chakra.

3

THE ROOT CHAKRA ALSO CALLED MULADHARA

This is the first chakra located at the base of your spine around the tailbone area. It is known as the Muladhara, which means the foundation or the root of all things. Muladhara breaks down into two Sanskrit words: Mula, which means "root" and Adhara, which means "support" or "base."

We are also told that Muladhara is the first chakra out of the three self-preservation chakras located on the lower half of the body. It is focused on your survival consciousness. Anytime we get anxious about our survival, this energy center is the one that gets affected the most. The Muladhara is responsible for your sense of safety and security on this earthly journey, so when you balance your root chakra, you create a solid foundation for opening all the other chakras above it.

How I like to describe to my clients is that working on this chakra can be likened to laying out the foundation for a house. The stronger and more solid that foundation is, the bigger, better, and more durable the house will be for years to come.

At some point in our lives, we've all struggled with a root chakra problem because the average human being has been subjected to some form of danger, pain, trauma, poverty, or abuse. Even if it was perceived danger, the energetic impairment still occurred. Those of us who have experienced the agony that comes with parents divorcing or if you were abused in any way as a child or if you lived in a location or a home where you never felt safe, then you certainly messed with your Muladhara chakra and unless you heal it, creating a permanent sense of safety and security in your world will be impossible.

Muladhara is our connection to the earth. It keeps us grounded and enables us to connect to our tribe and feel safe and secure. It is very important in helping us feel safe in the world.

The color associated with Muladhara when in balance: Red

The element associated with this chakra is earth. This chakra's animal totem is the snake according to Native American tradition or Elephant with 7 trunks according to Eastern Indian tradition.

If your energies are dominant in the Muladhara, then your main focus is food, shelter, sleep, and survival. The basic instincts that are necessary for survival are the most critical factors in your life. At this level or dimension of life, the only experience that matters to such an individual is basic survival and safety.

Responsible:

The Muladhara is responsible for basic survival instincts and feeling grounded.

Symptoms of an unhealthy root chakra:

If your root chakra is not functioning optimally, where the energy is blocked or not moving freely, you may find yourself feeling disconnected, anxious, worried, and feeling unsafe wherever you are.

Here are some other signs to look out for internally and externally:

- You tend to have trust issues.
- You're constantly preoccupied with feelings of uncertainty.
- You have a dysfunctional relationship with your family.
- You struggle with lower back issues, low energy levels, and cold extremities.
- You feel like there's not enough to go around and that you must always fight for what you want.
- Risk and loss terrify you.
- You often feel disconnected from nature and other people.
- You have a hard time just being authentically yourself around others.
- You're hyper-vigilant to any signs of danger from others or your surroundings.
- You're convinced that the only person you can depend on is yourself, and you struggle to ask for help even when you need it.
- You're constantly worried and anxious about money, perhaps to the point of obsession, so your relationship with money and how you handle or manage it is very poor.
- You're a hoarder.
- You panic a lot.

- You have low self-confidence.
- You have an unhealthy relationship with food.
- You struggle with decision making.

How many of these signs can you identify with on this list?

Triggers to become aware of:

Anything that shakes your sense of security can block the root chakra. Common examples include losing a job, business going bankrupt, and conflict with family members, spouse, business partner, or close friend. Divorce or relationship breakup. Receiving a troubling health diagnosis. Witnessing something horrific. Become more mindful, and you'll learn to spot the triggers in your life that shake up your sense of groundedness and safety. Then quickly work on getting it back into alignment.

Recently a client came in for a healing session. He is a successful man with a business that is steadily growing, but his obsession with money and the fact he always seems to be putting out financial fires that hinder the growth of the business led him to my healing table. Before we started doing the energy healing session, I wanted to understand more about his world and the framework he was working with. He told me how, in the past three months, he had generated $200,000 servicing his clients. Still, sadly, none was turning into long-term clients, and some were demanding their money back after a few months. So although money was coming in really fast, it was also going out really fast. This is a pattern he'd noticed for over a year. When it comes to his employees, it was no different. In digging a little deeper, I realized his employees were leaving because they felt he was delaying his payments, avoided salary conversations, and always complained to them about the poor job they were doing. He desired to be a millionaire, but his approach was very stingy, and money seems to get wings around him. If, like this man, you realize your relationship with money is unhealthy, healing your root chakra is one of the first things you must do before wealth can naturally flow to you. Many of us in society are unaware that the big financial crisis is actually an internal problem. There are those who quit a corporate job to become an entrepreneur because they believe this change will make them feel more secure about finances. The truth is, being an entrepreneur is a bigger risk than being employed. There is no such thing as financial security. So if you want to feel financial, physically, and emotionally secure, this is the foundational work that must be done regularly until that blockage is dissolved.

Another thing to remember is that because this is the foundational chakra, all the other chakras will work in better alignment when this one is unblocked and opened to optimum capacity.

Simple clearing exercises:

Stand with your feet parallel and at least shoulder's width apart. Keep your head floating above your body, chin tucked and spine straight. Rest your hands at your side then sink all your body weight and tension into your feet, allowing it to be absorbed into the ground. Now imagine roots growing out from the bottom of your feet extending deep into the ground beneath you.

As you do this, bring your attention to the root chakra and see a red ball of energy in front of your body. Visualize it moving back and forth and simultaneously vibrate the seed sound, which you will learn in just a bit until you feel that deep vibration and movement.

After the sound and vibration healing, you may also want to reinforce the new flow with some affirmations. Here are some good ones to integrate into your practice.

- I have all that I need, and everything is always working out for me.
- I am always safe, protected, and supported.
- I have a healthy body, a healthy mind, and an abundant life.
- I am stable, grounded, and relaxed at this moment.
- I am anchored to the earth and supported by the universe.
- I am secure and happy in my home, my work, and in my relationships.
- I am financially secure.
- My needs are always met.
- I claim good health.
- I claim abundance.

You also want to integrate the following into your lifestyle:

Exercise

Regular exercising to keep your body healthy and strong is vital for maintaining the alignment of this chakra. A body that is stagnant and not flexible helps to create a block in energy flow, so make sure you find a form of exercise that you enjoy. That can be running, Pilates, Yoga, Dance, Cross-fit, or whatever else you resonate with.

Daily sit outside and commune with nature

Simply relax and bask in nature, observing what's going on around you. Notice the birds, the wind, the light, the trees, the sun, or rain and just sense your interconnectedness with it.

Regularly practice "earthing."

Earthing is the practice of recharging your human energy field with that of the earth. This is done by walking barefoot on the grass or earth for the purpose of grounding, reconnecting, and recharging yourself. It is extremely useful, especially when you feel blocked in this chakra.

Getting enough sleep

Most of us are sleep-starved in the name of hard work and success. Ironically, the more you chase after that money and work hard, the more elusive success becomes. The idea of being wealthy and successful has gotten a bad rap in our society because, more often than not, it's been done out of greed, insecurity, and fear. More often than not, success comes at the expense of good health. These are all the basic results of individuals who are running around with dysfunctional chakras. When you learn to take care of yourself and keep all your chakras inflow, you will be able to create the wealth and success you desire. More importantly, you'll get to enjoy it. Sleep is a big determinant of how aligned your mind, body, and spirit is. Take the time to figure out what optimum rest is ideal for you and prioritize getting enough sleep. It will be beneficial for your body, your chakras, and your ambitions.

Design a diet that nourishes your body

Shortly I will be sharing examples of the types of food that you can incorporate daily when looking to open or unblock your root chakra. Given that this chakra is fundamentally focused on survival and your basic necessities of this material world, being more intentional about what you feed your body will enable you to keep it in alignment. The diet industry is a billion-dollar industry, and everyone has an opinion over what your meal plan should look like. Instead of giving you a rigid plan that you will soon give up, I want you to love yourself enough to design a lifestyle plan rather than a short-term diet plan.

Focus on choosing foods that you will eat daily, which you believe are good for you not based on what a book said, but based on how your body responds when you eat it. Make this a dialogue between you and your body. Start with simple foods. The more natural and unprocessed it is, the better it is. So choose foods that make your body feel good, make it a lifestyle, and you will never again struggle with eating right for your body type.

Meditation Techniques

Chakra meditation techniques are a great way to bring your chakras into alignment. The difference between regular meditation and a chakra meditation is that we focus on one specific area of the body. Here are the steps for the root chakra meditation.

First, sit with your back and spine straight. Relax all your muscles as you close your eyes and take in deep breaths. Inhale through the nose and try to pull the breath as far down into your body as you can. Exhale through the mouth.

Next, I invite you to turn your attention inward and downward to the location of the root chakra, right around your tailbone area. Notice any tightness around there. Since the color associated with the root chakra is red, I want you to imagine a red glow or spinning vortex that is deep red in color at the base of your spine. Allow this glowing light to expand all around that area and spread down toward the earth. Feel its warmth. Relax in this present moment and enjoy that emerging sensation for about 5 minutes. When ready, slowly come out of it, open your eyes, and sit in that silence for a moment or two before continuing with your day.

Daily Yoga

There are many yoga postures designed to cleanse and align this chakra. Finding time daily to do a little yoga either in the morning or before bed if it helps you relax and sleep is something I strongly encourage. Don't feel pressured to do an hour of yoga if your lifestyle cannot support this kind of commitment. In today's technological world, you could even join an online class like Udaya.com or Yogadownload.com and do ten-minute stretches and poses during your lunch break at the office. My favorite is the tree pose. It's one of the simplest poses to do anytime, anywhere, even if you're a complete beginner. To do it, firmly plant your entire left foot onto the floor, mat, or earth and bring your right foot up resting on the side of your calf muscle. Keep your hips pointed squarely ahead, and your toes tucked in. Be creative and make your tree pose your own by adding a little sound therapy or visualizing "red" glowing energy around the base of your spine. You can also play around with the location of your right foot and raise it or lower it, depending on your flexibility. Your arms can stay in prayer position, or you could raise them overhead, but remember to keep the base of your neck soft and elbows straight if you do. The most important thing here is to have the experience of feeling supported and connected to the earth. Do this for five to eight breaths and then switch sides.

Yoga Poses to help you feel grounded:

Triangle Pose, Child's Pose, Lotus, Garland Pose, Malasana Pose, Janu Pose Tree Pose.

Tools for balancing the root chakra

Crystals and Jewelry:

There are four traditional root chakra stones. Red Jasper is linked to balancing.

Red Carnelian, which is a great one if you're struggling with fear.

Obsidian which a black gemstone that is linked to protection. By wearing it, you may protect yourself and draw comfort, especially if in an environment that feels threatening.

Bloodstone is green with red spots. It is a semi-precious stone that is linked with pushing away negative energy and increasing self-confidence. You can also consider wearing red rubies.

Essential oils and aromatherapy scents like Sandalwood, Rosemary, Cypress, Cedarwood, Black pepper, Patchouli, and Vetiver. You can put these oils into an oil diffuser, rub them on your wrist, wear them in a diffusing pendant or sprinkle on your pillow before you go to sleep.

Nutrition:

Red foods like raspberries, cherries, tomatoes, and red bell peppers.

Root vegetables like beets, radishes, onions, garlic, potatoes are also great for grounding because they all grow in soil.

Protein-rich foods like tofu, green peas, spinach,

beans, and almonds also help to ground you and provide physical strength.

Spices like hot paprika, cayenne pepper, chives, dandelion, burdock, and horseradish.

Sound therapy:

Mantra Seed Syllable For Root Chakra: LAM

Finding stability in the physical world:

Start by making the necessary conscious changes that will enable you to feel safe, secure, and stable in the physical world. We cannot grow or reach the level of spiritual enlightenment our souls desire if fear cripples us. So make sure your home, your body, and your work environment feel safe and stable.

That doesn't necessarily mean forcing external things to become what they are not intended to be. Instead, it is an invitation to assess yourself, reflect on your state of mind, and become aware of the perspective and beliefs you hold that make it hard for you to feel safe and secure.

The same way a tree needs roots, your human aspect needs to feel a physical anchor in this world. Without those roots, your world is shaken by fear and anxiety, making it impossible to relax and find inner peace. Our bodies are designed to go into fight, flight, or freeze mode whenever we feel unsafe and unstable. This impedes our growth and makes it hard for us to bloom in all areas of our lives.

You have a right to exist and to be here on planet earth. Your maker desires you to be here. That alone should make you think and feel differently about your current life circumstances. You also have the right to enjoy the fullness of life and provide for yourself. In our society, that means a steady source of income, a job you enjoy, a roof over your head, clothes, mental stimulation, and whatever else you define as necessary to human growth. So never feel guilty about your desire for money, security, and a good life, these are your birthright. Instead, start finding ways to make yourself less dependent on circumstances when it comes to your sense of stability and provision.

There are already a couple of things you are doing that can help heal your root chakra if you bring in more mindfulness. For example, whenever you focus your attention on your body, you're creating space for grounded energy to heal you. That's why doing something like Yoga, body massage, or stretches are highly encouraged. As you do, these things bring in more intention and mindfulness to ensure that chakra energy flows in.

You can also bring in more mindfulness and attention to other physical activities such as cooking, gardening, painting, drawing, or dancing. If you are already doing any or some of these activities, take that time to acknowledge your root chakra. Whenever you acknowledge your thirst, hunger, need for sleep, or warmer clothes, you're also connecting and reclaiming your birthright to exist and enjoy the fullness of life. Have the intent to use these moments to align and connect with the energy of life and your root chakra, and it will turn daily activities into opportunities for alignment.

Here's another short exercise you can do on a weekly bases to ensure you're not neglecting this chakra.

Reflective questions to ask yourself:

1. Do I feel safe in my body? In my home?
2. Am I working in an environment where I can thrive?
3. What do I fear?
4. Do I feel like all my survival needs are met?
5. Do I have a connection with my body? The

planet? Life? If not, what can I do to strengthen it?

Try this now:

Take three deep, slow breaths and slowly repeat in a deep hum the mantra LAM with every slow exhale. As you do, bring your focus to the tip of your nose because the sense organ that corresponds to the root chakra is smell. If you do this well, you might actually feel your entire body, including the lower part, vibrate. This brings energy, blood flow, and all the essential good stuff into that root chakra to help balance and keep it in alignment.

The psycho-spiritual statement associated with this chakra is: I Have.

4

THE SACRAL CHAKRA ALSO CALLED SVADHISTHANA

The sacral chakra is the second major chakra of this seven-chakra system. In Sanskrit, it is called the Svadhisthana chakra, and it is your passion and pleasure center. The word Svadhisthana can be translated as "the dwelling place of the self."

It is located in the pelvic area (just below your belly button) and functions as the energy center for your sense of wellness, abundance, pleasure, joy, and -creativity. This is also our social chakra.

It helps us curb our controlling behaviors and find balance in our lives. When in alignment, it helps us recognize that acceptance and rejection are not the only options in our relationships, and we are better able to maintain healthy yin-yang existence.

A lot of people nowadays call it "sex" chakra. Why? Because the sacral chakra is considered the house of sex. This is the area where our most base desires and natural sexual urges spring from. The idea then is to help this chakra partner up with our heart chakra for the best outcomes. Working independently of the heart is unnatural and would be detrimental for the individual in the long run.

The sacral chakra is responsible for the energy coming inward into your body, and water circulation. Anything to do with the fluids in your body, as well as your reproduction, is regulated in this energy center. That includes physically, psychologically, and spiritually.

It is the womb area, the point of connection with others, feelings of intimacy, or desire. When people are violated of their sexuality and experience any kind of intimate or sexual trauma, this energy center becomes significantly affected. The results are often a very depressing disconnect with the physical body, which can be very confusing to the emotional body, but it can be healed.

Did you know the opposite of addiction is connection?

Those of us that turn to addiction do so because we lack the ability to connect intimately with others and ourselves in a healthy way.

This is the second of the self-preservation chakras.

The color associated with Svadhisthana when in balance: Orange

The element associated with the second chakra is water, which equals cohesiveness. The energy of the sacral chakra is feminine, passive, and lunar. This chakra's animal totem is the Dolphin according to Native American tradition or Makara (mythical crocodile) according to Eastern Indian tradition.

If your energies are dominant in your Svadhisthana, then your dominant focus will be to seek out and experience pleasure. This doesn't just mean sex, although it does include that. Instead, I am referring to every kind of sense of pleasure that appeals to you. You will be a person that loves to enjoy the world.

An individual who is a pleasure seeker obviously lives more intensely than a person who is living only for food, sleep, and basic survival needs. As you can see, these are different intensities of life. The more one increases in his or her ability to live from higher dimensions of life, the more focus and experiences also move.

Many teachers also portray the Svadhisthana as the system's petri dish, the soul where rich creative and original ideas are planted and nurtured within the individual. Meaning this is where you need to start looking if you want to start harvesting a more creative version of yourself. You must learn to go within and tune into your feelings, desires, dreams, and passions.

Responsible:

The Svadhisthana is responsible for reproduction, creativity, emotions, social connection, and all kinds of pleasure.

Symptoms:

If your sacral chakra is not functioning optimally, where the energy is blocked or not moving freely, you may find yourself struggling with impotence or infertility issues. Maybe you experience cramps or other menstrual problems. Perhaps you're feeling numb or overly sexually active or too frigid and cold. Some people struggle to feel any pleasure or desire. All these are symptoms that something is out of balance.

Here are some other signs to look out for internally and externally:

- You get easily offended and feel emotionally unstable.
- Frequent boredom and lack of drive and motivation to pursue anything.
- You fear change.
- You struggle with envy and jealousy.
- Addiction. This can be unhealthy use of drugs and other stimulants but also addictive behavior like excessive gambling, sexual compulsion, shopping, overeating, binge-watching, etc.
- You struggle with guilt and shame.
- Lack of creative inspiration.
- You don't feel passionate or thrilled by anything.
- Low energy and fatigue.
- You feel like a victim of circumstances and often find yourself trapped in cycles of abuse.
- Lots of allergy problems.

- You always wish you were somebody or somewhere else.
- You struggle with constant self-judgment and a feeling of never being good enough.

How many of these signs can you identify with on this list?

Triggers to become aware of:

Anything that inhibits your creative expression or makes you feel less than worthy and loved can create a blockage in your sacral chakra. Common examples include an abusive relationship (any kind of abuse), toxic people, or environments to mess with your creativity, thoughts that you're not good enough, and old painful memories from your past.

As living beings, part of our divine nature is to co-create with life. This co-creation can be expressed as procreation but is certainly not limited to baby-making. Many people only think about sexual intercourse when learning about their Svadhisthana. This is very limiting as they end up missing out on the countless other ways they could ignite passion, pleasure, creativity, and keep this energy center at optimum levels.

When you cook, paint, write, or grow flowers in your garden, you are co-creating with life. That is a creative act that nourishes your sacral chakra. Whenever you take any kind of raw material, either physical or mental, and transform it into something new and valuable, you are using your creative energy. In doing so, you are activating and aligning the power of your second chakra. That's why it's so important to immerse yourself in creative acts even when others don't get your "art". Anything you create that is coming from the depths of you will always be a masterpiece.

The key to opening your second chakra:

If you want to open and balance your sacral chakra, you must lose yourself in childlike play once again. Allow yourself to play. Remember how you used to build sandcastles, or Lego towers or color? It's time to let yourself take creative risks without the fear of failure. When you were small, you didn't care if the crayon went over the lines, why does it matter if your project isn't perfect now? That doesn't mean your career is over. Like the little you who was learning to walk, or ride their bike or color with crayons, you can start again right now. You have an infinite amount of creative energy within you - learn to use it in creative play.

Simple clearing exercises:

Sit in a comfortable position, keep your spine straight, and try to be as relaxed as possible. Take a few deep breaths. Now imagine a throbbing or swirling ball of luminescent orange light three inches below your belly button.

Feel the ball of orange energy dissolving all blockages (if you like, you can see it in the form of water ripples) and now start to see it moving from the front of your body to the back. Visualize it going back and forth and simultaneously vibrate the seed sound, which you will learn in just a bit until you feel that deep vibration and movement.

After the sound and vibration healing, you also want to reinforce some affirmations. Here are some good ones to integrate into your practice.

- I feel connected.
- I am creative.
- I love my sexuality, and it is vibrant.
- I feel complete peace from within.

- I am radiant, beautiful, strong, and in touch with my feelings.
- I love and approve of myself.
- I attract like-minded people who support and love me.
- I feel safe enough to express my sexuality in healthy ways.
- I feel worthy of receiving pleasure and having my needs met.
- I allow my feelings to move through me and release the need to suppress them.
- I release the need to self-medicate with any addictive substance or behaviors.

You also want to integrate the following into your lifestyle:

Drink Plenty of Water

This chakra is associated with the element of water, so naturally, the more hydrated you are, the better it will function. Make sure you are drinking enough plain water throughout the day.

Practice self-care and self-love

Daily practice of loving and appreciating your body, your mind, your dreams, and choosing to nurture yourself will realign your sacral chakra. Look at your body naked in front of the mirror each morning before you get dressed and generate feelings of love and appreciation. Touch and caress your body all over, honor your body, and feel joy inhabiting it.

You can also give yourself special treats frequently, such as buying yourself flowers, taking yourself out for dinner, etc.

Exercise

Regular exercising to keep your body healthy and strong is vital for maintaining the alignment of this chakra. A body that is stagnant and not flexible helps to create a block in energy flow, so make sure you find a form of exercise that you enjoy. That can be running, Pilates, Yoga, Dance, Cross-fit, or whatever else you resonate with.

Include play

As I said earlier, you need to allow your inner child time for play. And you also need to stop taking yourself so seriously when approaching new projects at work. Give yourself permission to be curious, have fun, experiment with new things, and enjoy the process even if it doesn't come out perfect.

Spend time near water as often as possible

If you don't live by the sea or ocean, you can make it a point to regularly visit whatever large body of water is closest to you. This can be a lake, river, waterfall, etc. And if that doesn't happen too often, use your creativity to innovate by either taking warm bubble baths or whatever appeals to your senses and feels pleasurable. Being around water is excellent for opening up and aligning your sacral chakra.

Get a journal for practicing gratitude and recording your thought process

Encourage your mind to think creatively and write down the thoughts that often dominate your day. Give yourself some direction on the topic and allow yourself a few minutes of writing every day. You can also do devotional writing, gratitude, and appreciation or even come up with poetry. Taking time to journal is a very healthy way to connect with your creative flow.

Make sensual and sexual activities valuable and sacred to you

Choose to walk away from the shame filled beliefs around sex and lovemaking and instead train yourself to enjoy and appreciate these activities. So whenever you're getting or giving a massage to your partner, making love, dancing, or taking baths together, use this time to deeply connect with the spiritual side of your nature and welcome the sacred energy from your second chakra.

Yoga Posses to help you get aligned:

Goddess Pose, Pigeon pose, Warrior II

Tools for balancing the sacral chakra

Crystals and Jewelry:

Moonstone, especially the peach moonstone that is linked to stimulating the mind and reducing worry. It also carries a kind of loving energy that can be very soothing. Orange calcite is linked to enhanced creativity. It also improves your mind-body connection.

Citrine stones, commonly referred to as "stones of the mind" are golden yellow in color. They are ideal if you're struggling with feelings of envy, jealousy, and low confidence as they are linked to increased self-esteem and confidence.

Carnelian is a semi-precious gemstone with a

reddish-brown hue and is linked with creativity and artistry.

Essential oils and aromatherapy scents like Orange, Rose, Grapefruit, and flower essences such as Lady's slipper and Hibiscus. You can put these oils into an oil diffuser, rub them on your wrist or wear them in a diffusing pendant.

Nutrition:

Fruits - Oranges are not only the same color as the sacral chakra, but they also share a strong connection and healing properties for this chakra. Be sure to consume those as often as possible. But don't limit yourself here. Any fleshy fruit is considered suitable for maintaining the alignment of this chakra. That includes mangoes, peaches, papayas, passion, fruit, etc.

Clear liquids - Teas and broths are believed to have healing properties that positively impact your sacral chakra, so treat yourself to a tasty vegetable broth or fruit tea when you need it.

Seeds - Any seed is said to be good for your sacral chakra, including pumpkin, sunflower, almond, walnuts, sesame, and poppy seeds.

Other types of food that unblock your sacral chakra include coconuts, which are said to increase your energy levels and trigger your creative flow as well as sweet potatoes and salmon.

Herbs and spices like vanilla, cinnamon, sweet paprika, coriander, gardenia, licorice, and carob.

Sound Therapy:

Mantra Seed (Bija) Syllable For Sacral Chakra: VAM

Making space for your emotions:

If you've been conditioned to deny, suppress, neglect, or downplay your feelings, then it's time to make a change. Many of us grew up in environments where authoritative figures taught us that emotions are a sign of weakness or that it is somehow wrong to show your true feelings because it might be inappropriate. Unfortunately, this type of thinking has done you more harm than good. Many of our problems in life are heart issues, and the only way to resolve them is to embrace all our emotions, both positive and negative. Choosing to be open and vulnerable about your emotions is not a bad thing. It doesn't make you less of a man or a crazy woman. Our society likes to dismiss emotional intelligence, but I assure you, your emotions have a bigger impact on the quality of your life than you may have been led to believe.

If you struggle feeling or identifying your emotions, it's hard for you to set healthy boundaries. It's also hard to understand how the universe communicated or how the results of your life are created. Can you see why this is a major problem?

Therefore, it is time you realize that feeling something is a good thing always. In the same token, experiencing pleasure is also a good thing. Granted, we may be seeking that pleasure sensation in harmful ways, but that doesn't make the actual desire wrong. As a spiritual being having a human experience, you have an unconditional right to feel and become aware of your emotions, learn to process them in healthy ways so you can better understand others around you, and you also have the right to experience pleasure.

There are already a couple of things you are doing that can help heal your root chakra if you bring in more mindfulness. For example, whenever you acknowledge how you feel in any given situation, you are making space for the energy of this chakra to flow in and heal you.

Feel your feelings. Do not censure yourself when you feel either high frequency (positive) or low frequency (negative) emotions. It might feel awkward at the beginning, but the more your practice processing all emotions, the more mastery you'll gain until eventually, you'll be able to simply observe them without attachment.

Here's another short exercise you can do on a weekly bases to ensure you're not neglecting this chakra.

Reflective questions to ask yourself:

1. Do I feel sexy and attractive?
2. What brings me pleasure?
3. In what areas of my life am I creative?
4. Do I feel sexually fulfilled?
5. Can I easily manifest my desires?

Try this now:

Sit in a comfortable position with your arms and legs uncrossed. Using your hand, touch your navel area and use circular clockwise motion as if you are winding the energy from your second chakra. Take a deep breath in and slowly exhale with the mantra VAM. Use the tone of your voice to engage that vibration and keep your attention on the reproductive area. Do this for three to five minutes.

You can also do some hip circles and make a figure of eight as that helps create an instant flow of energy. And if you really want to go wild on this, consider getting a hula-hoop.

The psycho-spiritual statement associated with this chakra is: I Feel.

5

THE SOLAR PLEXUS CHAKRA ALSO CALLED MANIPURA

This is the third of the self-preservation chakras. It is called the Manipura, which means the "lustrous city of jewels" or "seat of gems." Many teachers will also refer to it as the solar plexus or navel chakra.

Manipura is associated with inner satisfaction, serenity, self-assurance, willpower, and purposefulness. It has to do with digestion, personal power, laughter, anger, and ego identity. I'm sure you've heard the term "trust your gut." Well, this is the energy center that enables you to trust in yourself. When you know what you want, and you have a strong will, this is the energy center that's operating in full power.

Since this chakra is located near the abdomen (about two inches above your navel), it affects many of your internal organs including your kidney, pancreas, and intestines. Stomach ulcers and weight problems are usually due to an imbalanced Manipura chakra. For many decades I struggled with chronic intestinal ulcers. I saw various specialists and did countless tests, which didn't yield any positive result. The best response I could get was "because my ulcers were so severe and ran in my family lineage (in-fact killed my grandfather), it was doubtful that I would ever go a day without medication and a strict diet. There was very little I could eat without stirring up digestive problems and many times I passed out from too much pain. After I got married, however, and we decided to have a baby, I made the stern conclusion that I would find a cure that didn't include surgery to cut off parts of my inner organs and block some of the natural acids being produced. I didn't want to carry a pregnancy and bring into this world a baby incubated in years of daily medication. So in my quest to discover a permanent cure, I realized that healing my ulcers was directly related to my energy centers and spiritual body. The physical agony I had grown so accustomed to affected my emotional and spiritual states, and the more I learned to listen to and heal my body, the more I was able to heal my emotions and increase my spiritual connection. I also realized that I was holding on to a lot of emotional baggage and a lot of Anger. When you hold on to anger (and I know many of us have good reason to feel angry about something in the past), you throw your entire energy system out of balance. I'm going to share with you why anger is actually terrible for your body-mind-spirit connection in a few minutes, but here's the point I want you to remember as we study this chakra, your personal power, or lack thereof is directly determined by how healthy and in-flow this chakra is. So if anything is creating a block or causing it to not function optimally, you will struggle to feel and know that you can accomplish your objectives in life.

Have you noticed how easily distracted people are in today's world?

Many people are setting big goals, yet few actually achieve them. According to the University of Scantron, 92% of people who set New Year's goals fail to meet them. Only 8% of the population are actual goal achievers. If you look around social media, there are countless videos and articles on increasing productivity. Why? Because too many people struggle with maintaining focus and working on something until it's done. My conviction is that part of the problem in our society is that we are living an outside-in approach to creating success. Our inner work hasn't been done, and so the aspects of us that are meant to power us up and propel us into success are not functional. One such aspect is the solar plexus chakra, which is intended to empower you to focus and follow your chosen path without getting distracted.

The color associated with Manipura when in balance is: Yellow.

The element associated with the solar plexus is fire. It is meant to ignite your fire and strengthen your digestive fire. This chakra's animal totem is the bird according to Native American tradition or Ram according to Eastern Indian tradition.

If your energies become dominant in Manipura, then you are what we call a doer in the world. You want to make big things happen. Taking action is what matters to you, and you enjoy the feeling of power and control.

Responsible:

The Manipura is responsible for metabolism, digestion, personality, willpower, identity, and ego.

Symptoms:

If your solar plexus chakra is not functioning optimally, where the energy is blocked or not moving freely, you may struggle with ulcers, diabetes, hypoglycaemia, and other digestive issues. All gut issues arise from an imbalance of this chakra. A lot of stored emotions such as pain, trauma, sadness and grief can be lodged in the solar plexus.

Here are some other signs to look out for internally and externally:

- You often feel powerless and weak.
- Self-forgiveness is really hard for you to do.
- You struggle with feelings of insecurity and low confidence.
- There's a lot of unresolved guilt about the past that stays very activated in you.
- You tend to seek approval from others.
- You have excess weight around the stomach area i.e., a potbelly.

How many of these signs can you identify with on this list?

Triggers to become aware of:

The two most common triggers that lead to a blocked or weak third chakra are rejection and criticism. That includes perceived criticism and even the fear of possible rejection. Become more mindful of how your body reacts and what happens to your energy whenever you find yourself in these types of situations. If you notice a heaviness building up or nausea, immediately step back and distance yourself from it. If you're able to do a clearing exercise at that moment, that would be ideal; otherwise, create time to unblock and bring back into alignment your solar plexus.

For many of us, bringing this chakra into alignment will take several energy sessions and daily practice because the blockages run all the way back to childhood. In such cases, be kind and patient with yourself. The transformation will take place, but it may take time before you can fully manifest the new powerful you in your daily reality. This is an experience one of my clients had not too long before she came to work with me.

Sally had been studying and working on herself, energetically for several months. She picked up my yoga class to further enhance that healing. Somewhere along the way, Sally got a little impatient because she felt it wasn't translating into manifested reality as quickly as she'd hoped. When doubt set camp in her mind, she walked right into a situation that tested her new understanding. A man that she was deeply fond of rejected her after their first dinner date. She felt he was her soulmate, but of course, he strongly disagreed and didn't fail to let her know of his feelings or lack thereof. This one act of rejection sent Sally into a downward spiral of old hurts and memories of her childhood experiences of rejection, her feelings of "not being good enough" and being unlovable.

One afternoon after our yoga session, she opened up to me about what was happening and the fact that she was thinking about giving up her yoga practice because, in her words, "this stuff doesn't work for me."

After learning of the situation, I encouraged her to take up an energy session with me to see if it would help alleviate her current suffering and insisted that if after that session she was still convinced that these things don't work, she wouldn't have to pay a dime or continue attending my yoga classes.

We did an energy healing session. I had a chance to

listen deeply and uncover some of the hidden layers she hadn't been able to realize on her own. This became the turning point for Sally.

Like many self-help students that are doing it on their own, she was planting all the right seeds, but they were getting choked up by the weeds that still covered her beautiful garden. That's why it seemed as though nothing was working. Sometimes we need a little extra help and support from someone outside the picture-frame to help us spot some of those blind spots.

One of the critical lessons she learned that day is that deeply rooted beliefs sometimes require patience, compassion, and a lot of repetition before new ones can solidify. But as long as one keeps pouring in new energy, that flow eventually changes reality.

It's time to awaken and strengthen your fire:

The Manipura chakra is associated with the element of fire because ancient teachings taught of two fires resident within this chakra in all of us. Tejas and Agni. Tejas is meant to help you strengthen your inner fire, and Agni is intended to help you strengthen your digestive fire. Let's dig a little deeper into each.

Your Inner Fire:

You have a fire within known as Tejas in Sanskrit. In Aryuvedic teachings, this is known as the dosha Pitta. An individual with strong Pitta has that inner drive and willpower, which propels them forward toward their goals. But even if this isn't your dominant type, you can still harness the power of Manipura chakra to assert your will in a healthy, holistic way that empowers you to achieve any goal you set out to accomplish.

I encourage you to set clear goals, write down your desires, and daily step into your activities with intention and purpose. Each small step taken toward your set objectives will help strengthen your solar plexus chakra. Remember, the third chakra is full of power and intelligence that surpasses logic, and sometimes it is wise to tap into your "gut" feeling, especially if you're struggling with a decision.

Your digestive fire:

Agni is present in the Manipura chakra to help keep your digestive processes healthy. If you want to aid reigniting your Agni, I encourage you to hydrate more with plain natural water. If you are the dosha type called Pitta in Ayurveda, please avoid spicy foods. Other things that will help give you a more powerful Agni include drinking beverages at room temperature or slightly warmed as often as possible. You are also encouraged to take small sips of water while eating and avoid alcohol, fruit juices, or soda. That is because drinking a lot while eating tends to dilute the digestive acids, and of course, alcohol tends to produce excess acid, which all weakens your Agni. You may also want to give your stomach plenty of rest between meals to ensure your Agni is replenished.

If you are having trouble with your metabolism and digestion, you can quickly awaken your solar plexus chakra with simple breathing exercises. Here's an example of a breathing exercise you can try just remember to do it on an empty stomach.

First, you'll need to sit comfortably with the spine erect and shoulders relaxed. Then take a few deep breaths in and out through the nose with your lips closed.

Second, forcefully inhale through your nose while inflating your lower abdomen like a balloon and then forcefully exhale through your nose while pressing the lower belly toward the spine. It can be a bit uncomfortable the first time you try this, so don't let a little discomfort discourage you.

The key thing is to use a rapid pace, almost like an abdominal workout. Use one-half count on the inhalation and one-half count on the exhalation. Remember, it's always through your nose with the mouth closed. For beginners, we recommend no more than 10 repetitions, but if you've been doing it for a while, you can go up to 20 reps. The final outcome we are aiming for is a tingling or glowing feeling around the navel.

Simple clearing exercises:

Stand tall with your feet hip-width distance apart and make sure your spine is erect. Take some deep calming breaths in and out. Let's start by doing a few twists - side to side. Try to focus your attention on your midsection as you do this and make those twists as intense as your flexibility allows. You can raise your arms parallel to the ground if that feels good. Do this for about thirty seconds.

Now imagine a bright yellow ball of energy in front of your body just above your navel. Visualize it moving back and forth and simultaneously vibrate the seed sound, which you will learn in just a bit until you feel that deep vibration and movement.

After the sound and vibration healing, you also want to reinforce some affirmations. Here are some good ones to integrate into your practice.

- I trust my own guidance.
- I choose to live in a joyous present moment.
- I am magnetic to success.
- I can accomplish any objective I set for myself.
- I am worthy.
- I am brave and courageous.
- I am comfortable being in my power.
- I have high self-esteem.
- I am inspired and moved to get things done.
- I always use my power for good.
- I embody confidence and inner peace.
- I am in touch with my authentic power and control.
- I enjoy taking care of myself and setting healthy boundaries.
- I am responsible for my life and all my actions.
- I am powerful.

You also want to integrate the following into your lifestyle:

More sunbathing time

Now that we've learned the solar plexus chakra is represented by the element of fire, a good habit to get into is to spend a few minutes sunbathing each day. This doesn't mean by the beach in your bathing suit cooking yourself for hours. It simply means spending between five and fifteen minutes in direct contact with the sun. Taking a simple morning walk in the sunshine or relaxing on your patio with a cup of tea are just a few examples. If you live in the city and have a hectic life working behind a desk from 7am to 7pm then consider taking a ten minute break at some point during the day and either standing next to a big window when the sun is shining directly on your face or walk outside directly under the sun for a few minutes then get back into your to-do list.

Exercise

Regular exercising to keep your body healthy and strong is important for maintaining the alignment of this chakra. A body that is stagnant and not flexible helps to create a block in energy flow, so make sure you find a form of exercise that you enjoy. That can be running, Pilates, Yoga, Dance, Cross-fit, or whatever else you resonate with.

Work on your mindset

Mindset is everything when it comes to reclaiming your personal power and accomplishing your goals. Many of us are carrying around a victim mindset. This is one of the most damaging things for your solar plexus chakra. When you carry this mentality that you are defenseless, powerless, and a victim of circumstances, you cut yourself off from the boundless power of life. Whenever you find yourself blaming something or someone for anything, stop and work out the root cause because that thinking will only manifest more harm than good. If you're in the habit of saying people take advantage of you, that's also a sign your mindset needs an upgrade because all these thinking patterns only work to cut you off from your authentic powerhouse.

Eliminate toxic people and toxic relationships

Anyone who drains your energy criticizes you or belittles your ideas needs to be avoided or entirely eliminated from your list of friends. If you aren't able to cut ties entirely due to familial or professional obligation, be more diligent when around these people and make that interaction as brief as possible. Find supportive groups, either online or offline, that help you build up your self-esteem. Remember, you have to be completely responsible for your life. You have the power in your hands, and no one has the right to make you feel undeserving of anything good that you desire. Find people who uplift you and make it your intention to uplift others as well.

Regularly challenge yourself to step out of your comfort zone

We are creatures of habit, and in today's world, it can be all too easy to get stuck in a rut. Encourage yourself to step out of your daily routine often, even if that means driving to a different part of town for your weekend shopping. Seek out new experiences, set a big goal for yourself this year. Something that you know will stretch you and isn't easy to accomplish. By removing yourself from the comfort zone or things that are familiar to you, you will create a space for this energy center to supply you with power beyond what you thought possible. It might be scary at first, but trust in yourself and trust that life has your back.

Yoga Posses to help you get aligned:

Lion Pose, Bow pose, Boat Pose, Seated Spinal Twist, and Warrior.

Tools for balancing the solar plexus chakra

Crystals and Jewelry:

Citrine is believed to energize and open the solar plexus chakra by stabilizing emotions and dispelling anger.

Amber linked to aiding the body to heal itself by absorbing and transmuting negative energy into positive energy.

The tiger eye is also great for opening and activating the solar plexus chakra. It is also linked with balancing the yin and yang.

Essential oils like Rosemary, Clary Sage, Lavender, Clove, Sandalwood, and Cypress. You can put these oils into an oil diffuser, rub them on your wrist or wear them in a diffusing pendant.

Foods

Yellow vegetables and fruits like yellow peppers, yellow capsicum lemon, butternut squash, bananas, pineapple, and corn.

Complex carbohydrates like oats, brown bread, wholegrain cereal, and brown rice are great for giving you a steady supply of energy and aiding to keep this chakra inflow. Drinking Chamomile tea regularly is also recommended to help heal the solar plexus and it can also help settle an unsettled stomach.

Herbs and spices like lily of the valley, celery, anise, turmeric, fennel, cinnamon, and ginger.

Mantra Seed (Bija) Syllable For Solar Plexus Chakra: RAM

Learning to take responsibility for your own life and building up your willpower:

It is time to reclaim your full power. Take action for yourself, keep yourself accountable, and expect that you are capable of achieving whatever you set out to do. We all have ideas, dreams, desire, needs and yearnings but most of us lack the courage to materialize them. Is there something you've always wanted to have but struggle to believe you can have it? Is there someone you'd like to get acquainted with but don't dare approach them? It's time to step up your game and change that mindset. You are worthy, capable and good enough to have, be, do and give what you want. No longer stand on the sidelines of this movie called your life waiting for a hero to come and turn your story around. You are the hero, and everyone else should play a supporting character. Making this shift is challenging, and it will require a lot of courage, but as you learn to connect with your energy centers, ground yourself and trust in your divine nature, you will find a way to stop settling for a life that isn't worthy of your greatness.

Reflective questions to ask yourself:

1. Do I have a sensitive stomach?
2. Can I stand up for what I believe in?
3. Do I take full responsibility for my choices?
4. How do I handle poor feedback?
5. When was the last time I fully trusted in myself?

Try this now:

Lie down in a comfortable position and just allow yourself to be fully supported by the floor, mat, or bed. With your index and middle finger, physically try to locate your solar plexus so that you can know where to focus your attention for the next five minutes. To locate your solar plexus move two fingers above your navel, and you'll be able to touch on a very sensitive area, which you've probably noticed when you get nervous or had digestive problems. The first time I located it, I had an aha moment because I realized I was always touching that area whenever my ulcers would spur into activity, not knowing what they were trying to tell me. Once you feel connected to your solar plexus, relax your arms back to the side of your body, and let's do some energy healing.

Take a deep breath and create enough space in your body then focus your attention on your third chakra. Close your eyes and picture a vibrant, glowing sun. Now imagine breathing the sparkling warmth of sunshine and feel it entering your solar plexus and then exhale it back out. Feel yourself radiating, just like the sun. This sun represents your inner strength, intuition, and resources. Allow it to grow brighter and stronger. When you're ready, come out of this practice and step into your day feeling powerful and serene like the sun.

The psycho-spiritual statement associated with this chakra is: I Can.

THE HEART CHAKRA ALSO CALLED ANAHATA

This is the fourth Chakra in the seven-chakra system. It is known as Anahata in Sanskrit or the heart chakra. Anahata means, "unstruck" or "unhurt," which implies that beneath all the grievances of past experiences lies a pure and spiritual place where no hurt exists. That is what this chakra helps you reconnect with once again.

Anahata is the meeting point between the lower three and the upper three chakras. It is the point where the physical and the spiritual aspects of you are said to meet. The symbolism commonly used for the Anahata chakra is two triangles meeting (upward moving and downward moving triangles) because these are two different dimensions of life. The lower dimension caters to self-preservation, and the upper half caters to the longing to break free and go beyond.

This chakra is located at the center of the chest and includes the heart, cardiac plexus, thymus gland, lungs, and breast. Anahata chakra is responsible for giving and receiving love.

The color associated with Anahata when in balance is: Green. The element associated with Anahata is: Air

This chakra's animal totem is all Mammals according to Native American tradition or the Antelope according to Eastern Indian tradition.

Did you know as a human being, you have the power of unconditional love?

The heart chakra is the center for unconditional love. It governs your circulatory system, respiratory system, arms, shoulders, hands, diaphragm, ribs, thymus gland, etc. Are you starting to see where many of your physical ailments come from?

Whenever this chakra is underperforming, we are bound to manifest physical symptoms in one or more of those areas. This is why self-love, self-acceptance, and self-healing are some of the most critical tasks we each have to tackle. Unless we can first heal and bring back into alignment our heart chakra, it is impossible to heal another or make the world a better place.

If your energies become dominant in Anahata, then you become a very creative person. At this level, creativity flows naturally, and you experience life a little more intensely.

Responsible:

The Anahata chakra is responsible for compassion, love, trust, forgiveness, and equanimity.

Symptoms:

If your heart chakra is not functioning optimally, where the energy is blocked or not moving freely, you may feel as though your heart is hardened, shut down, numb, or blocked. You may struggle with feelings of loneliness, fear, lack of compassion.

Here are some other signs to look out for internally and externally:

- You carry a deep sense of fear.
- Jealousy and envy really dominate your

mental space, and you struggle to genuinely feel happy for other people.
- You struggle to give and/or receive love.
- You have issues with your lungs or chest region such as asthma or heart-related conditions like poor blood circulation, high blood pressure, etc.
- Resentment and grudges are constant companions because you find it very hard to forgive.
- You feel emotionally isolated and alone, even if you're in a relationship.
- You're continually replaying or reliving your trauma.
- There's a constant sense of heaviness in and around your chest area.
- You lack empathy.

How many of these signs can you identify with on this list?

Triggers to become aware of:

Anything that causes you to withdraw, close yourself in or go on defense or protection mode is most likely going to mess with your heart chakra. Whenever you find yourself in a situation where you start feeling depressed, anxious, or disconnected from the world, it's time to step back and remove yourself from that environment. If you feel like you're carrying the weight of the world all by yourself, then by default, you need to do some work to unblock your Anahata because it means something triggered you to shut down and close yourself from the Energy of Life.

The main thing to audit right now would be the relationships that are most active in your life. Are your friendships toxic? Do you have a partner who is abusing you in any way (emotionally, mentally, physically)? If you experience a terrible breakup, any loss, or if you struggle to deal with something emotionally traumatizing that happened in the past, these could all lead to the blocked heart chakra, and you definitely need to heal yourself.

I recently came across a very heartfelt letter sent to Private Lives (The Guardian Magazine) that was, in fact, a cry for help from a woman who is clearly struggling with her heart chakra.

The woman said, " I was in a relationship for five years. I adored him. It was very passionate, but we fought a lot too. I was always afraid he would leave me for someone, as he had a lot of female friends. I was worried about one girl in particular, and we fought about this. He would call me crazy and paranoid. So I gave him space to prove I trusted him -but then he broke up with me, saying he needed to be single and didn't want to be with anyone for at least a year. We tried to be friends. I foolishly thought I could win him back.

Six months later, he admitted he was with that girl, but that it had only just happened. I do not believe this. It has been more than two years since we broke up and I still can't get over this hurt and betrayal. I feel like those years were a waste of my time, and the memories are tainted - I can't even look at the pictures. I have become consumed with anger, hurt, and anxiety that everywhere I go that I will bump into them. I haven't spoken to him in a year, but I know they are still together while I'm alone and miserable. I have worked on myself a lot the past two years, but how can I forgive them and move on when they are not even sorry? I feel like I will never be able to love again or trust." (Source: www.theguardian.com - I can't get over the hurt and betrayal I feel from my last relationship)

If you have experienced anything close to this

woman's story, then you certainly must work on healing your Anahata. Here's what I recommend.

Choose the essence of Anahata:

Like the woman in the story, some of us choose to live in the past, to replay grievances, and to cling on to the pain caused by parents, siblings, old loves, classmates, business partners or bosses. Maybe you've been there too. At some point along this human journey, we will find ourselves right smack in the middle of a situation that can only produce pain. But here's the thing. You get to choose what to do with that hurt.

Some people choose to try to hurt the other person back. Others get bitter and resentful, locking themselves in that poisonous prison and refusing to move forward, as is the case with the woman. When you make that choice, it is you who gets hurt the most. Not living from a place of Anahata is confining yourself to a prison of eternal pain, not because the other person hurt you, but because you have chosen to keep yourself in that reality.

When you encounter hurt and pain, you can choose to embrace your emotions, feel them fully, and then let them go. In fact, it takes more energy to hold on to them than it does to let them go. As you let it all go, you open your heart to new people, new experiences, and you learn to dive deep into that part of you that transcends all hurt and pain. The woman in the story acknowledges that she's angry, anxious, lonely, miserable, mistrusting. Yet, for two years, she's still unwilling to choose differently. By not living from a place of Anahata, she continues to live from a place of fear, ignorance, anger, hatred, jealousy, and loneliness, which represents a closed heart chakra.

Holding onto pain harbors negative feelings and cuts you off from opportunities of love. So I am inviting you to make a choice right now. The choice is simple - choose to let go.

Your mind and ego may argue for your past pain, hurts, and limitations, but I can assure you, it is as simple as choosing to let go and move on. Similar to how you can be carrying a heavy bag on your back and then decide to place it down, stand erect and walk away, I am inviting you to do the same with any emotional baggage you've been carrying around. This is where we fall back on the power of unconditional love.

Unconditional love is a creative and powerful

energy that will guide you through the most difficult times, and the good news is that you have it at your disposal whenever you need it. You don't need anything or anybody to gain access to infinite unconditional love. Turn your attention to it right now. Welcome it. Call it in and allow it to free you from all limitations, all fears, and all past hurt.

Simple clearing exercises:

Sit in a comfortable, relaxing position with your spine extended up toward the sky. Turn your attention inward, and for a moment, try to detect your heartbeat either by sound or sensation. Now picture a glowing green ball of energy in front of your body around the center of your chest. Visualize it moving back and forth and simultaneously vibrate the seed sound, which you will learn in just a bit until you feel that deep vibration and movement. After the sound and vibration healing, you also want to reinforce some affirmations. Here are some good ones to integrate into your practice.

- I am love.
- Love is the answer.
- I am wanted and loved.
- I forgive myself.

- Love empowers me to forgive instantly, completely, and unconditionally.
- I love others unconditionally.
- My heart is free from past hurts.
- I love myself, unconditionally.
- Love is my guiding truth.
- I love life.
- My heart is open, powerful, and balanced in giving and receiving love.
- I choose joy.
- I am creating loving, nourishing, and supportive relationships.
- I am calm and peaceful.
- I love and approve of myself.

You also want to integrate the following into your lifestyle:

Start a gratitude journal

Make it a daily ritual to spend some time daily, even if for a minute acknowledging the things in your life that make you feel good. Count all your blessings all day every day regardless of how big or small. There is great power in daily gratitude. Both science and spirituality have proven that a grateful person goes through a significantly different life experience than one who doesn't daily say, "thank you".

Practice forgiveness daily

If you're breathing and interacting with fellow human beings, daily forgiveness is a must if you want to keep your heart chakra aligned. When we forgive, we are not making that hurt or betrayal okay. We are merely releasing it so that it no longer has a hold on us. Forgiveness is about you, not the other person. While it is not always easy to do, you will never experience love and joy if you don't forgive those that mistreat and hurt you. As you discovered in the story I just shared of the woman who felt betrayed by her lover of five years, she is the one still hurting angry, miserable and locked out of the joy of love. Her inability to forgive him has locked her into that reality. And she will continue to suffer until she learns to forgive him and herself.

Rihanna shared a candid conversation with Oprah, where she disclosed that her abusive relationship with Chris Brown, which was all over media, hurt her a lot. And it took a while before she realized that she was holding on to unforgiveness and victim mentality, similar to how she was feeling about her dad. So she did the inner work, chose to forgive her dad, and in so doing, finally forgave Chris Brown. As a result, she felt liberated from that entire ordeal. Sometimes the present reality is a wound that is rooted in something that happened in our childhood, and forgiveness enables us to dissolve both past and present hurts.

Remember, forgiveness must start with you. Do some reflection and take note of how you've mistreated, neglected, or berated yourself. Write a loving letter to yourself, asking for forgiveness. Put all the mistakes and messes and "should haves" down on paper, and once you do, sincerely ask for forgiveness. Then either burn or tear that paper as a symbol of new beginnings. Next, write a letter of forgiveness to all who have hurt you very deeply. Often, we need to start with our parents, as we tend to hold resentment towards them. None of these people ever need to receive the letter. The act of you writing, releasing, and choosing a new beginning is all you need to accomplish the objective successfully.

Laugh more often

Not only does laughter help open up and heal your heart chakra, but it is also good for your heart organ. Dr. Michael Miller, director of the Center for Preventive Cardiology at the University of Maryland Medical Center, said, "we don't know yet why laughing protects the heart, but we know that mental stress associated with impairment of the endothelium, the protective barrier lining our blood vessels. This can cause a series of inflammatory reactions that lead to fat and cholesterol build-up in the coronary arteries and ultimately to a heart attack. The ability to laugh - either naturally or as learned behavior may have important implications in societies such as the U.S where heart disease remains the number one killer".

In other words, find something that makes you laugh daily, even if it's as simple as watching your favorite cat video on YouTube.

Daily breathwork

Most of us have forgotten how to breathe correctly. I know that sounds strange, but it's true. If you're always feeling rushed, overwhelmed, and trying to keep up with a to-do list that never ends, chances are you spend more time shallow breathing. Learning how to breathe deeply is vital to your well-being and aligning your heart chakra because whenever we take shallow breaths, we are not using our organs and life force at full capacity. There is a constriction, and I'm sure with a little mindfulness, you'll begin to notice the difference. The more oxygen and life-force you bring into your body, the better your metabolism functions, the more relaxed and calm you will feel. You can try pranayama techniques such as alternating nostril breathing to get yourself into the habit of deep breathing. Another simple practice you can try is setting a timer on your phone several times throughout the day, where you simply pause for a minute and organically slow down your breath. Focus on taking deep belly breathes for that full minute. It will make all the difference in how you feel as you step back into your day.

Show more affection and kindness

This can be in the form of giving more hugs, doing one kind act to a stranger daily, or surprising a loved one. Did you know hugging releases oxytocin, which is a chemical that calms down the entire body and acts as a natural antidepressant? Try to make time for some hugs daily, and sometimes, hug yourself too. Showing kindness and affection doesn't need to be a grand gesture. Be creative with this. Maybe leave little notes for your loved one around the house to find. It could also be leaving little notes for yourself from time to time.

Sometimes I write a loving sentence to myself

and place it on my winter coat at the beginning of spring knowing full well that by the time winter comes around, I will have completely forgotten it, and what a lovely surprise to see how much I love and accept myself at the next turn of the cold season. Simple things like this go a long way in redefining your relationship with yourself and opening up your heart to more love.

Daily meditation

Meditating daily even for five minutes with your attention placed inward on your heart chakra can help unblock and bring back into alignment this energy center. Meditation has also been scientifically proven to improve mental clarity, boost the immune system, give you a sense of peace and calmness.

Yoga practices

Regularly practice yoga either at home or by joining your local yoga studio. Stretching your body and reconnecting with your breath helps to unblock and open up all your energy centers.

Yoga Posses to help you get aligned:

Camel Pose, Bow Pose, Cow Face Pose, Fish pose, Cobra Pose, Cat Pose.

Tools for balancing the heart chakra

Crystals and Jewelry:

Emerald is green beryl that is linked to bringing awareness of the unknown to conscious thought. It aids in bringing forth bliss and love into your life and deepens your meditation practices.

Malachite is a green mineral linked with clearing and activating all chakras but especially the heart chakra. It is used to stimulate instinctive and intuitive reason and helps in making changes, especially when it concerns personal evolution.

Green adventuring is linked to vitality, energy, and inspiration. It's said to soothe painful emotions and to assist when bouncing back from emotional setbacks and obstacles.

Rhodonite is linked with helping one fulfill their potential. It dispels anxiety, promotes coherence, and assists in balancing yin/yang energies.

Essential oils and aromatherapy scents like Jasmine, Bergamot, Rose oil, Marjoram, Angelica, and Lavender. You can put these oils into an oil diffuser, rub them on your wrist or wear them in a diffusing pendant.

Foods

When it comes to food, think green and healthy, and you can't go wrong.

Green vegetables like kale, brussels sprouts, spinach, peas, asparagus broccoli, avocado, celery, lettuce, and Zucchini. Fruits like green apples, lime, guava, green grapes, cucumbers, and kiwi. You can also experiment with superfoods like barley, chlorella, matcha, and spirulina.

Vitamin C foods - strawberries, orange, and any other fruits rich in vitamin C are known to open the heart chakra. Consider combining fruits and vegetables to make super healthy smoothies.

Teas - Green tea is an antioxidant and also a great beverage to help open up and align your heart chakra. Don't forget to drink plenty of natural water as well.

Warm soups - There is anecdotal evidence that soups promote recovery from illness and give the immune system a boost, especially when chakras are out of alignment. Experiment with a vegetable soup such as creamy broccoli or onion soup.

Herbs and spices like rosemary, cilantro, basil, sage, thyme, parsley cayenne, and marjoram.

Mantra Seed (Bija) Syllable For Heart Chakra: YAM

Reflective questions to ask yourself:

1. What relationships current or past require healing?
2. Do I struggle with receiving love?
3. What do I need to forgive myself for?
4. Do I love and approve of myself wholeheartedly?
5. Am I empathetic?

Try this now:

For the next seven days, monitor yourself. Go on a mental diet where you do not criticize anything or anyone either verbally or otherwise. That includes yourself. I also want you to try smiling at everyone you see daily, even if you don't feel like smiling. Do this for the next seven days and keep track of how you feel and what shows up.

When it comes to a simple physical exercise you can do now to open up your heart chakra, stand tall with your feet hip-width apart and spine erect. Now take a deep breath in and silently or audibly say YAM three or four times as you exhale. Take your time with this. Next, I want you to begin with arms hanging by your sides and shoulders pressed down away from your ears. Gently squeeze your shoulder blades together, broaden the chest and then bring the arms behind the back and grip elbow to elbow. Visualize divine energy and blood flow coming into your chest area as you breathe deeply and focus on opening up and aligning your heart chakra. After a few reps, you should feel some warm, soothing energy around your chest area. See if you can face "inward" and find your Anahata.

The psycho-spiritual statement associated with this chakra is: I Love.

THE THROAT CHAKRA ALSO KNOWN AS VISHUDDHA

The fifth chakra is known in Sanskrit as Vishudha, which means the "soul's gate". It is the mediator between our internal and external strengths serving as the crossroads between the heart and the head; emotions and thoughts. Although it is the fifth chakra, it is also the first of the three spiritual chakras that we'll be learning about and unblocking as we move upward toward the top of the head.

Vishuddha is located at the base of the throat area and governs the anatomical regions of the thyroid, parathyroid, neck, mouth, tongue, and larynx. I see this fifth chakra as the energy center that is responsible for your communication. When in alignment, this chakra enables you to listen, speak, and express yourself in a way that brings about harmony and demonstrates authenticity.

Vishuddha allows you to accept and express your authentic voice and speak your truth. It's about self-expression and trusting your inner voice.

The fork on the road that we all encounter:

At some point in our lives, we've found ourselves at a crossroads, unsure about which way to go. The ability to choose is one of the greatest gifts we have as human beings. Unlike all the other animals, plants, and creatures on this planet, we have been given the superpower of choice. Through the choices we make, we get to define what reality we shall experience. A rose doesn't have a choice; it must be a rose no matter what for its entire lifetime.

A human being is unique. He or she can choose whether to be kind or cruel, positive or negative, good or bad, happy or sad. Our ability to choose, however, doesn't make us superior to the law of cause and effect. With every choice we make, a consequence (effect) must follow. Everything that you speak comes from a choice you've made, and it will carry corresponding consequences. Even if you choose avoidance and decide to suppress your anger or thoughts, that is a choice that will bear consequences.

Have you ever had an experience where a lump formed in your throat, either because you didn't know how to express yourself or because you felt stymied by someone? That experience was a sure manifestation that was triggered by a choice you made to doubt or not speak your authentic truth.

The Vishuddha chakra is our consciousness in speaking our authentic truth. It connects up to the ears as well, so it's about all communication, which includes both speaking and listening.

The color associated with Vishuddha when in balance is: Blue.

The element associated with the fifth chakra is ether or space, and the sense most influenced is hearing. This chakra's animal totem is the White Elephant according to Eastern Indian tradition.

It's time to break your silence:

If your childhood or a big part of your life was spent around people who made you feel unsafe, unheard, or invisible, at some point, you might have either consciously or unconsciously decided it's better to stay silent about things that matter to you. If you grew up with parents who berated your ideas, then you may have conditioned yourself to avoid sharing what's really in your heart to avoid conflict or embarrassment. In doing so, you stopped giving power to your inner voice. If you, like many of us, realize that you tend to suppress your feelings and avoid conflicts, then it's a given - your throat chakra needs healing. It's time you started speaking up. Of course, when we teach of speaking your truth, this doesn't mean you become a jerk and create enemies. That is extreme, and in fact, arrogance, shaming, and abusing others is a sign that your throat chakra is out of balance. When your chakra is aligned, you will confidently speak your raw truth, and it will always be in harmony with the Life-Force because this is an intelligent universe. Speaking from your center of higher consciousness will never create disharmony because Truth is always Truth. Our job is to get really good at filtering and to discern the difference between perceptual truth and fundamental truth.

Due to the fact that your mind is also influenced by the conditioned beliefs you received during your formative years, it is always good practice to question your convictions. The more you learn to connect from your higher self, the easier it will be to recognize the distinct difference in tone and nature between your ego voice and your Soul's voice.

The key point here is that an actual demonstration that your Vishuddha is aligned can be known only if the voice that is loudest internally and externally is that of your Soul.

There is a wise and ancient Sufi saying that I encourage you to take on and it instructs:

Before you speak, let your words pass through three gates.

At the first gate, ask yourself, "Is it true?"

At the second, ask, "Is it necessary?"

At the third gate, ask, "Is it kind?"

How the lower chakras prepare you for authentic self-expression:

It is essential to realize at this point that the more work you've done on your lower three chakras, the easier it will be to open up, align, and engage this chakra. Everything is interconnected. For example, when you align the first and second chakra, you'll notice a newfound sense of courage and safety.

Overcoming fear will be easier. As your third chakra comes into alignment as well, you'll feel an increased sense of personal power, higher self-esteem, and confidence. That creates the perfect inner environment for you to start expressing yourself. Then, when it comes to verbalizing your needs authentically and boldly, having your heart chakra aligned and functioning optimally will enable you to be truthful to yourself and others in a loving way. That is why I always encourage my students to work on opening and aligning each of the seven chakras in ascending order. Expressing your truth is very liberating, and you can do it without fear of causing harm. It just takes a bit of practice.

If your energies become dominant in Vishuddha, then you learn to trust more in your own thoughts than seeking validation or approval from others. You stop all self-doubt and self-criticism, and you become very open and vocal about your authentic truth and what you stand for. Above all else, you become an excellent and powerful listener. People always feel safe, heard, and seen when they come to you for counsel.

Responsible:

The Vishuddha chakra is responsible for all communication and authentic self-expression.

Symptoms:

If your throat chakra is not functioning optimally, where the energy is blocked or not moving freely, you may feel unable to express who you really are, or struggle to voice your needs. You might also suffer from laryngitis, upper respiratory problems, and lower sinus problems.

Here are some other signs to look out for internally and externally:

- You live with the sense that "people don't really know or understand the real you".
- Recurring sore throat.
- Your actions go against your words.
- You struggle to name your emotions.
- Stiff neck.
- You feel nervous when trying to share your opinion.
- Your voice frequently cracks or sounds thin.
- Erratic fluctuations in hormone levels.
- You are shy and timid around others.
- Public speaking is almost as scary as death.

- You find it difficult to be honest with yourself and others.
- Expressing your emotions in a healthy way is a big challenge.
- You seem to be attracting relationships that are restrictive, and that don't allow you to freely express your thoughts and feelings without criticism.
- You struggle a lot with the fear that people will not accept you for who you really are, which often leads you to downplay your ideas, needs, and desires.

How many of these signs can you identify with on this list?

Triggers to become aware of:

Anything that inhibits your ability to self-express and communicate authentically is going to create a block in your energetic body. This could be in the form of criticism from an authority figure or someone who influences your life, such as a parent, spouse, or business partner. It could also be in the form of verbal aggressiveness or abuse either in the workplace or at home. If you have a mother in law, a boss, or certain friend who don't respect your boundaries or "get you", it's very likely that they might trigger a misalignment if you're not mindful.

Many times we become too accommodating instead of saying what we want because we fear the rejection or conflict that might arise. In such cases, especially when it's someone you care about, it's crucial to begin making the shift toward self-expression by practicing out loud to yourself before approaching the person.

For example, I had a client last year that was coaching men on how to tame their inner animal. He came to me because he realized he needed some energy healing sessions to enable him to speak up and voice his needs and desires authentically.

Ever since David was a child, he had learned to downplay his desires because his mother always criticized everything he did. To appease her and be accepted as a good boy, he shut down his voice and always did what the women in his life wanted. He soon discovered that it was quite favorable. His mother always praised him for being quiet and never arguing back. As he turned into a young man and got into college, he realized getting into the company of women was very easy. They loved having him around, but there was one thing missing.

None of the girls ever saw him as a "boyfriend" type. He was always stuck in the friendship zone. Now in his twenties and with a psychology degree under his belt, he still has no deep romantic connection. When he came to the realization that he was scared of telling a woman "what he wants", something shifted in him. He knew the problem lay within not externally. The voice that he'd learned to mute out years ago needed to be unmuted and nurtured back. This is not always easy to do, especially if one is shy and introverted.

Aside from the healing sessions, I also tasked David with the assignment of practicing using his voice to cultivate the courage and confidence needed. I got him to write out the phrase he would say when he was with the woman he's been in love with (stuck in friendship zone) for the past five years. He started practicing this in front of the mirror twice a day while speaking out loud. At first, his voice would thin out and sound choky, but after a while, things got better. His palms stopped sweating, his voice became clear and deep, and he was finally able to make his desires known to her.

I fear many women have a blocked throat chakra when it comes to expressing their truth and ambitions because, for centuries, women were not allowed to speak. As such, this is one of the chakras that I encourage everyone to work on whether you think it's blocked or not.

Simple clearing exercises:

Sit comfortably in a chair with your eyes closed. Inhale and exhale for about five minutes, as deeply as you can. Breathe in through the nose and out through the mouth. Starting at the top of your head, perform a body scan (scanning the body from top to bottom, and imagining your muscles relaxing as you go.) Once you've done this and you feel completely relaxed, I want you to picture a glowing blue ball of energy in front of your body. See it spinning, glowing, and expanding in size right at the level of the throat. Visualize it moving back and forth and simultaneously vibrate the seed sound, which you will learn in just a bit until you feel that deep vibration and movement. Now allow that glowing energy to disperse throughout your body as you focus on a feeling of openness and relaxation in the throat. When you're ready, open your eyes and either sing your favorite song out loud or read something inspiring out loud for a few minutes.

After the sound and vibration healing, you also want to reinforce some affirmations.

Here are some good ones to integrate into your practice.

- I speak my truth, kindly, and clearly.
- I willingly release all fears, anxiety, and negativity that block me from speaking my truth.
- I communicate clearly with love and compassion.
- True power and freedom is when I listen to my inner voice.
- It is safe for me to express my ideas and desires openly.
- I lovingly and courageously allow my Higher Self to speak through me.
- I use my words to create beauty in this world.
- I use my voice to bring peace and love into this world.
- I express myself with confidence.
- I speak from a place of wisdom and compassion today.
- I honor my thoughts, ideas, and opinion.

You also want to integrate the following into your lifestyle:

Drink Plenty of healthy beverages

This chakra is associated with your throat and voice, so naturally, the more hydrated and relaxed your throat area is, the easier it will be to remain in-flow. Make sure you are drinking enough plain water throughout the day, as well as fresh juices and teas that help keep this chakra in balance.

Deep breathing into your stomach

This is a great way to ensure you don't end up speaking impulsively, nervously, or that you lose your voice. Before expressing yourself, get into the habit of grounding yourself first. Do this by breathing deeply into your stomach so that it expands gently. Focus on this sensation and allow it to center your energy and summon your confidence and authority.

Expand your listening skills

Train yourself to be a good listener when interacting with people. I also want you to become a good listener to your internal dialogue. When dealing with other people, pay attention to their body language, be attentive, and show the other person that you are actively listening by nodding, making small comments, and mirroring what they're communicating. Listening is an art, and there are many great resources that can help you improve this skill. On the resources page, you will find a recommended site that can enable you to master the art of listening.

Give yourself permission to sing out of tune

You may not have the voice of Celine Dion, but I still encourage you to sing to yourself as often as possible. It is a gentle way of opening up your throat chakra. If you don't want to sing around other people, then do it in the shower.

Daily spend time in silence

Taking some time daily, even if it's just five minutes to be in the silence can help you tune into your authentic inner voice. As counterintuitive as it may seem, going into the silence will benefit your throat chakra healing, as it will permit the rise of your inner voice. As your inner voice emerges, your throat chakra will strengthen. Ever wonder why Yogis often take vows of silence? Now you know. By going into the silence, they are able to communicate freely with their divine consciousness.

Read aloud

This can be a chapter from a book, an affirmation spoken daily in front of the mirror, or a passage from your preferred sacred scripture. I also encourage all parents to make this a daily habit for their little children as they grow up. Reading out loud helps one develop confidence, it helps with the practice of being assertive, and it opens up your chakra.

Yoga Posses to help you get aligned:

Plow Pose, Lion's Pose, Shoulder stand Pose, Fish Pose, Baby Cobra Pose.

Tools for balancing the throat chakra

Crystals and Jewelry:

Tanzanite is linked with activating the spiritual chakras, especially the throat chakra. It is known to facilitate communication with the spiritual realm and increase your will to express your truth.

Aquamarine is perhaps the most well-known throat chakra crystal. It has been linked with connecting an individual to his or her higher self. The crystal represents courage and acceptance. It provides emotional and intellectual stability. Using this will enable you to travel deep within yourself.

Lapis is a semi-precious stone linked with enhancing states of self-acceptance and serenity. Some call it the "stone of truth". It is said to improve communication and stimulate emotional, mental, and physical purity.

Kyanite is one of the few minerals that never require cleaning. It is known for aligning all chakras automatically and immediately. Using it for your throat chakra will help you open up, heal, and experience deep and meaningful meditations.

Essential oils and other aromatherapy scents like Yland Ylang, Peppermint, Spearmint, Eucalyptus, Clove, Neroli, Frankincense, and Myrrh. You can put these oils into an oil diffuser, rub them on your wrist or wear them in a diffusing pendant.

Nutrition:

Consider adding blue-green algae and kelp into your diet as often as you can.

Blueberries are the most potent foods for the throat

chakra. Other fruits that are also great for keeping this chakra aligned include apples, oranges, grapefruit, kiwi, lemons, limes and practically any other fruit you can think of that grows on trees because traditionally it is believed that such fruits represent authenticity since they only fall from their tree when they're ready to eat.

Liquids like water, fruit juices, and herbal teas.

Herbs and spices like salt, peppermint, sage, lemongrass, red clover blossoms, and coltsfoot.

Sound Therapy:

Mantra Seed (Bija) Syllable For Throat Chakra: HAM

Reflective questions to ask yourself:

1. Do I speak my truth?
2. How can I best use my voice to serve others?
3. Who in my life do I struggle to communicate with?
4. Are there topics or subjects that I get anxious talking about? Why is that?
5. Am I expressing myself creatively and what do I do to strengthen that?

Try this now:

For this exercise, I want you to be comfortable enough to use your voice. Find a place where you can speak aloud the mantra for the allocated time without being disturbed. You don't have to scream, but I do encourage you to speak up. Simply pick a tone and volume that feels loud enough for you. Take a deep breath, stand tall and confident, and on your exhale with your attention on your throat chakra repeat the mantra - HAM. Remember, this is a vocal exercise, so make sure you can hear your voice and follow your breath for the entire practice.

Do this three to five times a day for about 3 minutes. I like to visualize the clear blue sky in my throat chakra when I do this one and often repeat in the morning before starting my day and for a few minutes before I give any speech.

The psycho-spiritual statement associated with this chakra is: I Speak.

THE THIRD EYE CHAKRA

This is the sixth chakra that most refer to as the third eye. In Sanskrit, it is known as Ajna chakra, which means "beyond wisdom". Ajna is located in the space between your eyebrows at the center of your forehead. It encompasses the pituitary gland, head, eyes, and lower part of the brain.

Now please remember that the third eye doesn't literally mean a third human eye. As we said, these are energy centers, and this particular center helps you unify your thoughts and clearly see beyond the physical. Ajna is the domain for intuition, imagination, self-awareness, clairvoyance, telepathy, and manifestation as it helps to regulate wisdom and insight. The sixth chakra leads you to an inner knowledge that can guide you throughout your life no matter what you're dealing with if you let it.

This is where you focus on your meditation and visualization when you are designing your life. The Ajna chakra taps into what is known as divine seeing. When the mind is busy and distracted, it becomes impossible to see clearly. The third eye is the chakra most psychics rely on because they use this chakra to see beyond the physical realm; hence, the term "seers".

The difference between sense perception and spiritual perception:

Did you know that long before your birth, you were able to hear, listen, experience touch, taste, and even perceive light? Most of us have grown so accustomed to seeing, hearing, tasting, touching, and speaking through our physical organs that we've lost the ability to experience anything more than sense perception. Don't get me wrong, sense perception is wonderful for this human journey, but it is only a small aspect of what we can do as divine beings. The third eye chakra enables us to reconnect and perceive far beyond the physical through expanded spiritual awareness. I hope that by the time you are done reading this book, you will awaken and get back in touch with your ability to sense beyond the ordinary physical realm.

The color associated with Ajna when in balance is: Indigo. The element associated with the third eye chakra is light. This chakra's animal totem is the Black Antelope.

If your energies are dominant in your Ajna, then your main focus is Enlightenment. According to yogic philosophy, once the third eye is aligned and in harmony with all the other chakras, a doorway to spiritual enlightenment is opened. Such an individual possesses strong intuition, insight, self-awareness, and emotional balance. He or she sees life with great clarity just as it really is and strives for that oneness all the time.

The eye of the soul:

Many Yogis teach that the third eye is the "mother" of all other chakras, the eye of the Soul - and with good reason. The third eye not only sees, it also perceives the meaning of what is seen in the light of the soul. That is why you will find phrases like "seat of the soul" being attributed to the third eye chakra. When the third eye is aligned, we don't just see, we gain understanding. We are able to discern what is reality and what is an illusion.

In our current society, few are able to see clearly. That is perhaps why, as we advance, we are having more and more burnouts, depression, suicide, etc. I recently had a conversation with a woman named Caroline, who has been struggling to make her business work for the last five years. In probing a bit deeper into who she is, her vision for the business, and what she believes about herself, it became evident all her chakras required some deep energy work. Her Ajna has probably been blocked since she was about ten years old when she first experienced the feeling of reproach and demoralization. She shared two different occasions of her early childhood, where her parents scolded her for offering an opinion where none was asked. And she recalled her mother frequently saying that she must obey instructions without questions. In her twenties, she continually struggled with bouts of depression and anxiety, and today she's married to a man that she feels doesn't value her opinion or appreciate the work she does. For the past five years, she has been attempting to get her counselling business off the ground so that she can stop having to depend on her husband or work at his company because as much as she loves him and has no intention of leaving him "I feel suffocated and crippled by his close-mindedness and condescending remarks even in front of his employees. I sometimes feel like he treats me worse than the janitor even though I am a director of the company and his wife".

When one is faced with a situation like Caroline's clearing and realigning all the chakras, especially the third eye, chakra becomes imperative. If you realize your Ajna needs some work, one of the first things you'll want to do is reawaken your intuition so that you can start receiving the insights needed to make the right choices. That is something Caroline has never had. In all these years trying to find a way out and become successful on her own, she's not had any intuitive guidance, which meant all her decisions were blindly taken. She has found herself in some tough situations all because she made the wrong choices. In life and in business, there are certain cues that life gives us if we are tuned in, to help us avoid making unnecessary mistakes, but often we ignore or miss the cues altogether. Decision-making is an essential skill that every leader and successful business owner needs to have. Still, it doesn't come easy when one has a blocked Ajna. Caroline said she struggles a lot with decision making because she fears to make the wrong choice yet again and doesn't want disappointment. I know this is a common experience for many who have blocked chakra, so if that's you, follow the suggestions below, and you too can begin to initiate your unique process of the third eye chakra healing.

Responsible:

The Ajna chakra is vital for self-awareness, concentration, clarity, imagination, and intuition.

Symptoms:

If your third eye chakra is not functioning optimally, where the energy is blocked or not moving freely, you may have constant headaches and nightmares that affect your sleep. You could experience blindness, blurred vision, or other types of eyestrain. When your third eye chakra is blocked, it's hard to visualize anything. Your inner vision is impaired.

Here are some other signs to look out for internally and externally:

- Back and leg pain.
- You rarely feel inspired by anything.
- Your creativity feels muted out.

- Recurring sinus problems that are quite painful.
- You're emotionally reactive and get upset quickly.
- You have trust issues and tend to dislike people easily.
- Your interactions with other people feel very superficial, forced, or trivial.
- You find it hard to be open-minded.
- Your ego feels dense and heavy.
- Focus is a huge struggle for you.
- Your decision-making is extremely long, complicated, and strenuous, often breeding self-doubt and second-guessing.
- You're very attached to outcomes being exactly the way you want.
- You have rigid opinions about the world that you aren't willing to change.
- You're very fussy about details and getting things right but struggle to see the "bigger picture."
- You often get lost in your thoughts.
- You struggle with overwhelm and lack of clarity whenever something new comes up.
- You ignore listening to or often struggle to

understand when messages are from your intuition.
- You often experience a sense of a cloudy and foggy mind.

How many of these signs can you identify with on this list?

Triggers to become aware of:

Anything that inhibits your creativity, intuition, and imagination is probably going to lead to a blocked third eye chakra. Many of us have grown up in environments that blocked the energy flow of this chakra that we might not know what it's like to actually have it open and aligned. So perhaps with you, it's more a question of realizing that your chakra has always been blocked, and it's time to align it for the first time. If, however, you know what it's like to have your Ajna chakra in alignment, some of the triggers you might want to become aware of that mess with it include exposing yourself to conversations that make you feel insignificant or not worthy. You also want to catch yourself whenever self-doubt, self-criticism, self-loathing, and any other kind of negative inner dialogue begins, as these are poison for your third eye. Be very cautious of situations or people that trigger the fear of not being sure of yourself. That is one of the major blocks and the root cause of many of your sufferings in life.

Tuning into your inner guidance for help:

I am a strong advocate for "going within" to find solace, solutions, and peace of mind instead of relying on external sources. When it comes to doing what is right for you, nothing is more potent than training yourself to ask your inner knower. If you learn to ask the right empowering question and make yourself a receptive vessel, you will always receive a hunch or subtle feeling of moving forward or holding back in regards to that topic. This is your inner guidance system helping you navigate this journey of human life, and it is never wrong. It might take a while to strengthen that channel of communication, but I encourage you to work on it. Whenever you feel conflicted, ask for your sense of intuition to open and aid you in attaining the mental clarity and serenity needed to make the right choice.

A question I get asked so often by my clients is, "how can I be sure that the answer is really coming from my intuition"?

The simple answer to that question is - the more in

tune you are with yourself, the more you learn to trust and discern the voice coming from your Higher Self, the easier it is to know. It is a knowing. No one can give you that knowing or certainty. Only you can give it to yourself through practice. A great place to start when seeking to align and reconnect with the power of your Ajna chakra (and this might seem counterintuitive) is to focus more on healing and aligning your lower chakras. Sure, there are higher-level things you can do to heal your Ajna chakra, and I will share some of these practices in a few minutes, but I want you to realize that spiritual awareness is best experienced in this human form when the needs of the human form are satisfactorily met. In other words, you have to figure out what your needs are, find a way to meet them, and align those lower chakras so that all fear, anxiety, worry, self-doubt, insecurities can fade away. Only then is it easier to stop getting in the way of opening up to your divine nature. You need to understand that your Higher Self isn't lacking anything. There is no blockage or insufficiency or withholding on that end. All the power, joy, love, insight, wisdom, clarity, and knowledge you will ever need to be the highest version of yourself in this lifetime is already present and available here and now. But you may not have access to any of it.

Do you realize a person can die of starvation even though he is a millionaire? If he doesn't know that he's a millionaire or how to access those millions, he may end up dead in a ditch like a pauper. The same is true for us in receiving the spiritual nourishment we need. If we don't know how to access it, there's no way of enjoying it. Accessing it has more to do with having all the self-preservation chakras and the heart chakra open, aligned, and in perfect flow.

Once you have worked on the lower chakras and aligned your third eye chakra, you will find it easier to be objective and less fixated on your personal beliefs. As a result, life will take on a more vibrant quality, which will help you become more creative and spontaneous. You'll start to view life from a bird's eye view more often, which will give you wisdom and compassion.

I have had clients who went through the healing process and came out the other side transformed in ways beyond their expectations. One client, for example, developed the clairvoyance, and she reported feeling more timeless and boundless. It can be a very liberating and life-altering experience, so take your time, enjoy the process, and expect astonishing things to happen.

Simple clearing exercises:

For this chakra, we are going to do a simple mindfulness meditation as we clear out the energy. Start by sitting comfortably with your spine straight and relaxed. Inhale and exhale deeply and slowly for about ten reps. As you do this, bring your attention to the breath and watch it as it moves in and out three or four times, then shift your focus and pay attention to the area where the third eye is located. Continue to breathe slowly and deeply until all ten counts are done. Next, I want you to picture an indigo or violet sphere of energy in front of your forehead. Visualize it moving back and forth and then up and down. Picture the ball of energy getting bigger and warmer as it moves throughout your body, and as it does, imagine it purging negativity from your body. Feel yourself absorbing the third eye chakra's energy. If you like, you can also vibrate the seed sound, which you will learn in just a bit until you feel that deep vibration and movement.

After the sound and vibration healing, you also want to reinforce some affirmations. Here are some good ones to integrate into your practice.

- I am the source of truth and love.
- I am connected to the deepest aspects of myself.
- I am connected and guided by my intuition.
- I am open to visions of the imagination to flow freely in a positive light.
- I listen to my deepest wisdom.
- I know my own authentic voice, and I trust it.
- I have a healthy mind.
- I have clarity and understanding.
- I am spiritual truth.
- All the answers I need are within me present for me to receive.
- I am connected to my true path and purpose.
- I am connected to my own inner vision and trust it.
- I am true to myself, and I clearly hear the voice of my soul.

You also want to integrate the following into your lifestyle:

Spend time soaking in sunlight

The element associated with your Ajana chakra is light. As such, taking some time daily or as often as you can to soak in light will help open up this chakra. If you live in a dark or cold climate, consider trying light therapy. There are many benefits of sunlight, and as we shared earlier, even your third chakra benefits significantly from regular sunbathing. What you may not have known is that your third eye chakra is associated with the pineal gland (a pea-shaped mass within your brain), which is responsible for sleep and hormone regulation. By bringing in sunlight, you help awaken your pineal gland, bring more clarity into your mind, and heal your third eye chakra.

Self-reflection

Taking some time for quiet self-reflection is essential for personal growth and also for reconnecting with your Ajna chakra. This is actually considered a skill that you will need to develop over time, so don't worry if at first, it feels awkward or difficult to do. Start by journaling your thoughts daily. Do a regular self-assessment of your thoughts, behaviors, and the progress you're making. See how in tune and in alignment, all aspects of your life feel.

Mindfulness techniques and practices –

Take up some mindfulness practices and daily

experiment to see which one best suits and meets your needs. Here are seven that you can try today.

1. Mindful breathing.
2. Mindful awareness.
3. Mindful appreciation.
4. Mindful observation.
5. Mindful listening.
6. Mindful eating.
7. Mindful showering.

Daily Meditation

Daily meditation can have numerous benefits for our physical, mental, emotional, and spiritual health. Science has proven that even as little 15 minutes taken for daily meditation can reduce mind-wandering, increase focus, boost the immune system, and increase overall joy and well-being. When we meditate, we enhance open up and bring into alignment the third eye chakra, which enhances our focus, clarity, and decision-making skills. Researchers from John Hopkins University found general mindfulness meditation programs helped ease psychological symptoms from anxiety, depression, and pain related to stress. In general, meditation has been shown to improve sleep quality, increase pain tolerance and stabilize emotions, so as you can see, doing this daily will not just align your chakras, it will reinvigorate your entire body system.

Candle gazing

Hatha Yoga encourages and teachers what it called Trataka, aka candle gazing. It's a powerful way to open up your third way and develop your focus and concentration. Do it by lighting a candle, place it four feet in front of you at eye level, and gaze into the flame of the candle while incorporating mindful breathing. Keep your vision focused on the flame gently and naturally and notice the flow of energy within your body.

Regularly do yoga

Yoga stretches are a great way to reconnect your body-mind-spirit. That creates the harmony needed for all the energy centers to start functioning optimally. Consider joining your local yoga studio or signing up for an online class and do a few minutes of Yoga at home. Below are a few poses that are specifically good for the third eye chakra.

Yoga Posses to help you get aligned:

Child's Pose, Fish Pose, Shoulder stand, Yoga mudra.

Tools for balancing the third eye chakra

Crystals and Jewelry:

Sapphire, which can be blue, yellow, green, or red, is linked with releasing stuck energies. It's excellent for opening up the third eye chakra, especially the blue Sapphire. It will also bring you joy and peace of mind.

Shungite is linked with power and is believed to be a great shield. It will restore balance in your body, helping your third eye chakra to open and align.

Amethyst is a famous and beautiful precious stone linked to healing headaches and the third eye chakra. It is often used as a symbol of wisdom.

Purple Flourite is a semi-precious gem that is linked with sharpening intuition. It's one of the most ideal third eye chakra crystals, especially if you're struggling with a lack of clarity or need to become more decisive.

Essential oils and aromatherapy scents like Sandalwood, Rosemary, Patchouli, Frankincense, Juniper, Clary sage, and Vetiver. You can put these oils into an oil diffuser, rub them on your wrist or wear them in a diffusing pendant.

Nutrition:

Omega-3 rich foods such as walnuts, salmon, chia seeds, and sardines are great to add to your diet as they enhance cognitive function, which helps open up your third eye chakra.

Fruits and vegetables like blueberries, eggplant, purple grapes, blackberries, prunes, dates, figs, purple cabbage, purple kale, purple carrots, and purple potatoes are also potent for helping align your third eye chakra.

Dark chocolate helps enhance mental clarity and boost concentration. It also contains magnesium, which alleviates stress, and, as a bonus, it aids the release of serotonin, which elevates your mood, so if you enjoy dark chocolate, feel free to give yourself a treat frequently.

Herbs and spices like poppy seed, mugwort, juniper, lavender, eyebright, and rosemary.

Sound Therapy:

Mantra Seed (Bija) Syllable For Third Eye Chakra: OM

Reflective questions to ask yourself:

1. What do I believe in?
2. What is my purpose here?
3. When I honored my intuitive guidance or inner voice, what happened?
4. How open am I to other world viewpoints?
5. What or whom am I judging right now? Am I willing to relinquish the need to judge others and myself?

Try this now:

Take a deep breath in with your eyes closed, and the eyeballs slightly rolled upward and inward toward the pineal gland. Visualize the indigo color of the third-eye chakra. Then exhale with the sound OM. Play around with the tone of the sound until you find the specific one that makes you feel a vibration around your third eye. Do this for five minutes. Now grab a pen and paper and write down how you feel and what thoughts or ideas are showing up for you.

The psycho-spiritual statement associated with this chakra is: I See.

THE CROWN CHAKRA ALSO CALLED SAHASRARA

This is the seventh chakra and is the last of the seven-chakra system that we've been studying. It is called the Sahasrara chakra in Sanskrit, which is translated to mean the "thousand-petal lotus". This chakra commonly referred to as the crown chakra, is where we receive our divine knowledge, inspiration, and knowing. It's where we experience our divine self and the deep understanding formed by communing with the divine. Closely connected to the third eye chakra, it is associated with specific areas of the brain, such as the pineal gland, pituitary, the nervous system, and all master glands.

The location of this seventh chakra is at the uppermost tip of your physical body. In Tantric philosophy, we are taught that this is the point where spiritual introduces energy for distribution throughout the body. The crown chakra is the meeting point between the finite and the infinite. It is the seat of cosmic consciousness or divine awareness that connects each of us to the eternal Lifeforce. In thinking about and visualizing the crown chakra, we see it as located just above the top of the head.

It allows us to experience unity and oneness. It enables us to realize that everything is connected at a fundamental level.

Gaining true knowledge

Given that the crown chakra is all about transcendence, it makes sense that as one opens and aligns this chakra, many of the ego sufferings cease to exist. That doesn't mean your life becomes dull or that you stop increasing in knowledge. Instead, it means that an individual living in such a state seeks knowledge that helps him or her experience greater freedom and non-attachment from all known and limiting concepts. Meditation and silence would be very appealing to such an individual, but it wouldn't be used as a means for escapism or coping mechanism. It would be an effortless and enjoyable experience carried out in the name of passion and love of one's soul. Reality, perceptions, material manifestations would all take a different shape, and he or she would see things as they really are not through the lens of any limited belief system. Spiritual union and communion would be one of the most ecstatic experiences that go beyond anything ordinary human beings experience.

That good feeling that's unutterable is secretly what we all long for. It's the reason we smoke, drink, shop, gamble, and get addicted to sex. We can feel in our hearts that feeling ecstatic is good, but we seek that feeling in all the wrong places. We seek it in transient, external experiences instead of seeking it in the higher eternal realm. When your crown chakra fully opens up and aligns, you will find your infinite supply of ecstasy - the Holy Grail spoken of by many teachers.

Emerging as your true self:

Both Buddhism and Hinduism share this analogy of the lotus flower. The lotus flower is nurtured and emerges as something beautiful from an environment that contradicts its beauty. In other words, out of muddy waters, something beautiful, pure, and vibrant appears. The beauty possessed by the lotus is unique to its environment as it blooms where there is an absence of clarity and vibrancy. The point here is that you possess the same ability to rise out of the muddy waters and limitations imposed upon the true you. As the crown chakra opens and aligns, you can transcend the physical body, the ego-mind, and the intellect. You can even push beyond the individual soul that ties you to Samsara (the endless cycle of birth and rebirth). This is the gift that awaits those that go all in. That doesn't mean it will happen overnight. Going through this book doesn't mean you will gain instant enlightenment, but it will place you on the path and help you take the first step toward the rise and emergence of your true divine self.

The color associated with Sahasrara when in balance is: Violet and White. The element associated with the seventh chakra is thought. This chakra's animal totem is the Eagle.

When your Sahasrara truly opens, you receive the realization that you are pure awareness. You become one with pure consciousness, undivided, and all expansive. Like a drop in the ocean, you realize that you are part of that ocean that contains and encompasses every aspect of all that is known and unknown. This becomes the place you live from, boundless, timeless, and with a profound knowing and reverie for that which we call Life.

Responsible:

The Sahasrara chakra is essential for gaining deep understanding, clarity of self, and connecting with the higher self.

Symptoms:

If your crown chakra is not functioning optimally, where the energy is blocked or not moving freely, you may feel bored, off purpose, and disconnected from the source of your wisdom and existence. You might experience apathy, learning difficulties, lack of inspiration, depression, and other destructive behaviors.

Here are some other signs to look out for internally and externally:

- You lack faith or any spiritual grounding.
- Greed and materialism.
- You feel disconnected from others and life itself.
- Extreme egotism.
- You have a limiting self-identity.

- You're chronically exhausted.
- You have sleeping disorders.
- You feel a lack of direction and purpose.
- You struggle with loneliness.
- You're bored and fed up with life.
- You struggle with mental illnesses.
- Any talk of spirituality, Higher Power, God, or Enlightenment really puts you off.
- You struggle with recurring emotional imbalances and finding inner peace.

How many of these signs can you identify with on this list?

Triggers to become aware of:

Anything that inhibits your ability to connect with a higher level of awareness or higher consciousness can easily block your crown chakra and disconnect you from that divine flow. Often times, the common triggers that lead to a closed or blocked chakra include a daily work environment that is not conducive for you. Going to a job you hate will cause an imbalance to occur. Anything that forces you to accept things blindly, submission that comes from a place of fear and feeling inferior, feeling insignificant and undervalued as well as continually receiving false information can all trigger a block of your crown chakra. Something else to consider is the fact that when your lower chakras are blocked and you're in that state of disharmony, you will struggle to keep this chakra aligned because your mind will quickly get drowned by the fears, insecurities, and demands of your material world. Therefore, as mentioned before, work on your lower chakras, and you will have an easier time keeping this chakra aligned.

Don't let your ego get in the way of leading the life you were meant to have:

Ben shared his story with me right before our first healing session, which might be of great value to you, especially if you're struggling to overcome ego deficiencies.

"I have been fiercely independent my whole life, harboring the deeply rooted belief that I can handle anything, and I don't need help from anyone. But something happened to me a year ago that has caused me to realize I might have been working with a false framework for life. I let my own judgment and B.S cloud my perception for a very long time. I spent years thinking, "a woman can never cheat on me" until I caught my fiancée with another man in our apartment. Then I spiraled into a dark place, lost my job, and the woman I so desperately wanted to marry and ended up convinced that "women will always cheat on me". The pain and confusion of what happened to me made it impossible for me to logically figure out what was going on in my life. It's like my reality had been turned upside down, and everything was topsy-turvy. Food lost taste, the sky was always grey, and the world seemed to be tainted. I could feel myself falling fast into a very old yet familiar pit of depression that I had experienced once more during my twenties, and I wanted no part of it. Back then, therapy seemed like a better option, and it did help for a while. This time around, I needed a real cure and something that wouldn't end up in over the counter prescriptions. So I bit the bullet and went online. I started to interact with people who had similar trust issues and somehow pulled on the thread that led me to you. It had never occurred to me that I had always felt disconnected from myself and even from my partners. I had never connected the dots to see that I've ever had trust issues, and perhaps even some of my smug confidence came to compensate hidden insecurity. More importantly, I had never realized that my insomnia, reoccurring migraines, and frequent back pains were all connected. So when you said my relationships and my career snag are interconnected, I literally felt a heaviness in my chest, and my vision got blurred".

The realization that we've been living caged in a false sense of self with limited awareness is one that often doesn't come until a painful experience hits us really hard. Ben was no exception. As he went seeking truth and solace from an enemy he'd identified on the outside, he realized the real enemy was within all along. In learning to open up and align your chakras, the gift of higher-level consciousness is usually the key to liberation that helps you make sense of your past, present, and future life.

Our egos are usually the great obstacle standing in the way of that discovery, which is why many of us have to fall into that pit a few times. I don't know how many times you've fallen into your pit, but I hope after going through this book, you will never again experience that disconnect. Whether it's just recently happened or has been plaguing your life for years, now is the best time to make some new changes and watch for transformation.

Simple clearing exercises:

Sit with your back straight and feet on the floor. Place your hands on your lap and turn your palms to the sky. Gently close your eyes and inhale through your nose and out through your mouth. Imagine a bright violet or white ball of energy at the top of your head. Visualize it trickling from your head downward, flowing effortlessly. Sense it getting bigger and brighter as you continue to breathe deep and slowly. Feel it warming the crown of your head and allow that warmth to spread all the way down throughout your body. If you like, you can also vibrate the seed sound, which you will learn in just a bit until you feel that deep vibration and movement.

After the sound and vibration healing, you also want to reinforce some affirmations. Here are some good ones to integrate into your practice.

- I know the universe is friendly, kind, and loving.
- I know I am loved, protected, and prospered.
- I connect easily with Source Energy.
- My light attracts others that respect my unique vibration.
- I am here to make a difference.
- I know my own spiritual truth, and I live in accordance with it.

- I know my true worth and value.
- I am at one with the world around me.
- I am connected to my soul's purpose.
- I receive guidance from my higher self.
- I know I am one with the universe.
- I know I am worthy of love and all good things.

You also want to integrate the following into your lifestyle:

Find your spiritual outlet

We all possess spiritual gifts and talents that can be nurtured and cultivated to help us not only keep the divine connection but also share something magical with the world. For some, like me, it's writing. Others it's drawing, painting, composing music, poetry, dancing, playing an instrument, cooking, gardening, and the list goes on and on. What is an activity you do that makes you forget about time, location, obligations, etc.? Find that thing and do it as often as you can.

Spend time in prayer, devotion, worship, and thanksgiving

Daily prayer, worship, devotion, and thanksgiving

don't have to be a religious act unless you are religious. It is merely the natural and straightforward act of taking time to commune and appreciate the power that is breathing and sustaining you even as you read the lines on this page. Take time daily to bask in the joy that comes from connecting to this incredible power. That can be in the form of religious devotionals and worshipping rituals, or it can be as simple as watching a sunset, a sunrise, or the birds in the nearby park. Keep the simple statement "thank you" on the tip of your tongue as you do this, and you will feel an instant shift.

Daily meditation

Mediation is one of the most powerful practices you can integrate into your lifestyle to open up and align your crown chakra. It can be a guided or silent meditation, depending on your preference and level of experience. As mentioned earlier, the benefits of meditation have been scientifically proven, so it's not an exaggeration to state that this single change will transform every aspect of your life. From a spiritual perspective, mediation will enable you to unlock the door between your inner and outer world. It will connect you with your divine nature and the source of life. There are many forms of meditations, but as a beginner, experiment with the meditation technique I will share at the end of this chapter. If you want more comprehensive education as well as guided meditations I recommend checking out sites like The Chopra Center or Gaia.com

Be mindful of your ego

There is a distinct difference between self-confidence and egotism. Many of us are so accustomed to living purely from the ego-self that we confuse the two. Self-confidence and self-esteem are rooted in self-acceptance and higher knowledge of your true identity, while egotism, in most cases, is rooted in fear and insecurity. It is often the egos way of masking the feeling that it is not powerful, strong, and capable. The more you can learn to detach from your false identity and live from your true identity, the easier it will be for your ego to stop ruling your life. As you do, your crown chakra will align and open up in powerful ways.

Always choose peace and love in every situation

It's easy to be kind, loving, and peaceful when the situation is good. But when challenged with a problematic, unkind, or negative situation, few are able to cling on to Truth. If you want your crown chakra to serve you at the highest level and if you truly desire that connection with the supreme consciousness, you must find a way to tame your mind and become as the sacred lotus is portrayed. As mentioned before, the thousand-petal lotus is a symbol of this chakra, and we know a lotus emerges out from the most undesirable environments because it is unmoved by the murkiness of its surroundings. Your growth and evolution in this life are pretty much the same. The peace of mind you desire, the safety, stability, power, everlasting joy, and love cannot be contingent on your environment; otherwise, you will never know the truth about life.

I encourage you to start choosing love in your life. Start by loving yourself and seeing yourself as good in all circumstances and conditions. When you make an error in judgment instead of beating yourself up, lovingly acknowledge, learn, and move on. When you do something good, celebrate and reinforce your self-love. The more self-love you can immerse yourself in, the easier it will be to offer it to others even when they act like jerks. We are not capable of fully loving and accepting others until we learn to love and accept ourselves fully. The same applies to peace. When you choose to cultivate peace in your inner world, you will naturally find a way to live in peace with others in this outer world. There's no better way to open up and balance the crown chakra than continually reminding yourself that you are choosing peace and love in your life regardless of conditions.

Study spiritual teachings and cultivate a spiritual discipline

Incorporate yoga into your daily routine

Daily yoga helps you get in touch with your energy centers and channel more creativity, confidence, and joy into your life. In the resource section of this book, I will share different resources where you can go to see video demonstrations of the various yoga poses I have suggested. The take-home point for you when it comes to yoga is that it doesn't have to be time-consuming. As little as 10 minutes of intentional, well-executed poses daily executed will enable you to open up your chakras. What's great about doing yoga is that these poses not only help align and open up your crown chakra, they also help balance all the other chakras as well as your masculine and feminine aspects.

Yoga Posses to help you get aligned:

Headstand Pose, Lotus Pose, Downward-facing Dog

Pose, Lord of the Dance Pose.

Tools for balancing the crown chakra

• Crystals and Jewelry:

Amethyst is one of the most popular and beautiful crystals that range from deep violet to delicate lavender in color. It is linked with bringing calmness and serenity to mind. Use it to guard against physical and mental attacks and allow it to protect your spirit. It is believed to help activate the crown chakra opening new doors of possibilities, which can include increased wealth and prosperity. It also has the ability to assist in overcoming addiction and alcoholism.

Selenite is a clear mineral that is believed to open the crown chakra as well as the third eye chakra. Use it to help you build momentum and forward movement in your life, especially when things start to feel like they are stagnant.

Sugilite is a lavender crystal that is often called the love stone. Use it to guard yourself against negativity and to amplify your sense of spiritual groundedness.

Charoite or Chaorite Jade is a stunning stone that is linked with transmuting energies and grounding the spiritual self. It is used to assist one to face difficult choices and decisions bravely. Use it to build a connection between your heart and crown chakra. Allow it to protect you and your environment against all harm.

Clear quartz is a mineral linked to enhancing energy and clarity. Use it to boost your spiritual connection and as a tool to help you gain clarity on what you truly desire from life.

Essential oils and aromatherapy scents like Lavender, Jasmine, Cedarwood, Rosewood, Sandalwood, Spikenard, Myrrh, Galbanum, and Frankincense. You can put these oils into an oil diffuser, rub them on your wrist, wear them in a diffusing pendant or sprinkle on your pillow before you go to sleep.

Nutrition:

When it comes to food for this chakra, less is more. Ancients taught that fasting and breathwork is the best way to feed the crown chakra.

Of course, we all know the importance of eating, so when you are thinking about how to nourish your body in a way that helps you open up this chakra, choose pure foods that are grown in nature, absorbing natural sunlight.

Vegetables such as eggplant are recommended in your diet as well as fruits such as red grapes and passion fruit. Instead of sweets, opt for dried fruits like dates that are dried out under the sun. The more you can get away from processed and packaged food, the better.

Herbal teas like peppermint are also great for the crown chakra.

Herbs and spices like ginger, holy basil, Gotu kola, lavender, and lotus.

Sound Therapy:

Mantra Seed (Bija) Syllable For Crown Chakra: OM

Try this now:

Sit or stand in a comfortable position and imagine your crown chakra opening as you breathe in deeply and exhale with the seed mantra OM. Repeat this practice for at least five minutes. You may also choose to sit in the silence and place your attention on the chakra.

The psycho-spiritual statement associated with this chakra is: I know.

MORE TOOLS TO OPEN AND HEAL ALL YOUR CHAKRAS

Now you have an in-depth understanding of each of the seven chakras and how to open and realign them. Remember, yoga and meditation are considered the best tools and techniques you can incorporate into your daily life to heal and align your chakras. Besides that, there are other tools and activities you may want to use in everyday life to accelerate the healing process.

Massages:

Using the massage technique to open up and heal your chakras has become quite common. Below is the method for each of the chakras.

The Muladhara - Massage the gluteal muscles, legs,

and feet. That encourages energy flow (prana) to circulate in the region of the Muladhara or root chakra.

The Svadhisthana - Massage the hip region. Myofascial release, along with the releasing of the iliopsoas muscle, will help relieve tension in the hips, which opens up that energy flow to the Svadhisthana or sacral chakra.

The Manipura - Massage the abdomen area using clockwise motion around the navel. Applying essential oils here is highly recommended. Simply pour some on your palm and enjoy a nice gentle massage with conscious intention until you feel that sense of upliftment and increased personal power. It also encourages waste elimination and improves organ functions as energy begins to flow in the Manipura or solar plexus chakra.

The Anahata - Massage the area of the upper back and the gentle traction to the shoulder joint and arm. This aids in the opening up of the chest area and the Anahata or heart chakra.

The Vishuddha - Gently massage the back and front of the neck. Follow it up by gently massaging the areas connected to the base of the head as well as the base itself to allow the full energy flow of the Vishuddha or throat chakra.

The Ajna - The best and most commonly used massage technique for Ajna or the third eye chakra is known as "brow stripping", which includes the muscles in the jaw area, temples, and nasal sinuses.

The Sahasrara - A gentle, tranquil massage you can give yourself to open up the flow of energy into your Sahasrara or Crown Chakra is tapping the middle of your scalp gently. You can also give yourself a full scalp massage followed by hair pulls and cervical traction to release cranial-tissue adhesion.

Color Therapy:

The energy relating to each of the colors associated with the seven chakras can be worn or visualized upon to help bring about a sense of alignment and harmony. Try incorporating these into your everyday life as outfits especially when you feel like you need to emphasize and reconnect with a particular chakra.

- The Muladhara aka Root Chakra – Visualize and wear Red.

- The Svadhisthana aka Sacral Chakra – Visualize and wear Orange.
- The Manipura aka Solar Plexus Chakra – Visualize and wear Yellow.
- The Anahata aka Heart Chakra – Visualize and wear Green.
- The Vishuddha aka Throat Chakra – Visualize and wear Blue.
- The Ajna or Third Eye Chakra – Visualize and wear Indigo or if that's a bit hard to shop for consider shades of purple.
- The Sahasrara or Crown Chakra – Visualize and wear Violet as well as pure white.

The science of the chakra system

Is there scientific proof for the existence of energy centers, aka the chakras that are found within us?

In 1975, Dr. Robert Ader presented an explanation of an experiment that provided the first scientific evidence that our thoughts actually alter our immune system. Over one hundred years ago, Sir William Osler wrote about a patient who had an asthma attack after smelling an artificial rose. In the mid-1970s, Dr. Ader provided the scientific explanation for Osler's curious observation when he demonstrated that mammals are capable of conditioned (Pavlovian) immune responses - that is, Ader's scientific studies effectively used thoughts and emotions to mediate changes in the immune system of the physical body. His findings were profound as until recently, each body system was considered to function in a pristinely independent manner. He revealed that everything is connected and emotional stress indisputably and negatively impacts our physical health. (NIH)

Science may not directly prove the existence of the chakras yet, and there is still much debate in the academic world around the human body and mind, but we do know that science agrees that everything is made up of energy. All matter is held together via energetic bonds and consists of atoms, of which most is empty space. The movement of energy is vital to life. When we think, breathe, make any activity, and even while at rest, electrical energy is flowing through our bodies via our neurons and nerve pathways. Based on the experiments conducted by Dr. Ader and many others as well as what quantum physics has now been able to confirm about energy, we may not be able to prove it scientifically, but we can feel the truth in these ancient teachings.

Many of these ancient traditions did come from primitive understandings of biology. Therefore, I encourage you to keep an open mind, continue to educate yourself, and maintain a degree of flexibility when trying to understand the meaning of their teachings.

More practical tips to experiment with:

Aside from meditation, yoga, and other already mentioned tips that you can incorporate into your lifestyle for opening up and healing each of the seven chakras, here are some different ways for you to move energy, unblock and heal your chakras.

- Reiki therapy.
- Energy healing work.
- Acupuncture.
- Tantric energy work.
- Kundalini massages.
- Kundalini yoga.
- Tapping techniques.
- Music therapy.
- Tai Chi
- Feng Shui

AFTERWORD

With all that we have learned throughout this book, it is essential to realize that chakras are not "things" but energy centers. And as spiritual seekers and students of life, we must avoid becoming too rigid in our thinking so as not to block our spiritual evolution. Depending on the experiences, exposures, mentoring, training we've had, or what we've read, heard, seen, and been told, we hold a particular view of the chakra system.

In different traditions, you might find flowers, animals, animal parts, geometric shapes, deities, Buddha's, yantras, wheels, or mandalas all attempting to express their version of the same truth. The one thing you must refrain from doing as you move forward in your practice of yogic philosophy is to avoid emotional reactivity, for that is a sure way of blocking your chakras. Train your mind to explore, to be curious, and to entertain the concept of paradoxes for such is the nature of life.

Even if your chakras feel dormant right now, trust in the natural unfolding process of your life. Inactive chakras are energetic potentials in the same way a bud is the possibility of a flower. I recently bought tulips that had not yet bloomed, and I placed them in a vase on my kitchen table with nourishing water and recommended nutrients then patiently waited. On the morning of the second day, several of them already started blooming. By the third day, my kitchen was beaming beauty from all the tulips that were nowhere in sight only a few days ago.

Begin to think of yourself the same way. The true completion of a flower in bloom can be considered the absolute state, a naked state of the essence of that flower. If left undisturbed under the right conditions, the next stage of unleashing potential is inevitable. As with the flower, a dormant chakra when given the proper care and nourishment must bloom and mature.

The subtle body

By now, you have been introduced and reacquainted with your subtle body. Remember, we are all in possession of this subtle body. It is the subtle body that perceives sensation, so when amputees feel phantom pain in missing limbs, you can be sure they are receiving communication from their subtle body. It is also the astral and dream-state vehicle. Tantric systems such as Japanese Shingon, Tibetan Buddhism, and Taoism view the subtle body as a vibrationally refined aspect of the physical body, central to spiritual evolution. Non-tantric traditions such as Zen Buddhism see the subtle body as secondary and instead endeavor to confound logic so higher forms of understanding become a bit more accessible. In her Lion's Roar review of "Religion and the Subtle Body in Asia and the West," Lama Willa Miller writes, "In contemporary Tibetan Buddhist practice, the subtle body acts as a kind of bridge between the body and mind. This view can be found dating back to the work of Yangonpa Gyaltsen Pal (1213-1258), a Tibetan yogi and author of one of the earliest Tibetan handbooks describing the subtle body." Regardless of how you choose to align with this concept of a subtle body i.e., tantric or non-tantric tradition, the fact of the matter is that you'll have an easier time opening up and aligning your chakras when you develop a working understanding for yourself. We see the subtle body as the context for knowing and working with the chakra system just as the physical body is the context for organs and the circulatory system.

When you fully open your chakras, they disappear like knots removed from a length of silk thread. Paradoxical as it may sound at first, this perspective is congruent with the chakra teachings that perceive the system as a verb instead of a noun, a concentrated energetic activity instead of a luminous colored Frisbee. The starting point is the basic visual teaching of a wheel, but once you get to the point of full alignment and opening, the systems, channels, and points operate as a unified conscious energy field.

By going through this book, you have taken the first step on this journey. As you diligently move forward in your spiritual evolution, you will bloom and mature until you reach your absolute completion. What is absolute completion? It is the absolute, open complete state of creative potential where "blooming" disappears, leaving only free-flowing nadis and fields of energy. May this book aid you in meeting that desirable end.

RESOURCES

Guide To The Chakras For Beginners And Healing Practitioners. (2019, July 25). Retrieved October 31, 2019, from https://www.chakras.info/

Lion's Roar. (2018, May 16). Retrieved October 31, 2019, from https://www.lionsroar.com/reviews-investigating-the-subtle-body/

Kundalini Massage – Your Key To a Remarkable Source of Energy And Power | Chakra Healing - All About The 7 Chakras. (n.d.). Retrieved October 31, 2019, from http://www.chakrahealing.com/kundalini-massage/

Raise Your Vibration With These Colors | Chakra Healing - All About The 7 Chakras. (n.d.). Retrieved

October 31, 2019, from http://www.chakrahealing.com/raise-your-vibration-with-these-colors/

80 Easy Forms of Chakra Balancing for Mind-Body Healing ⋅ LonerWolf. (2019, April 13). Retrieved October 31, 2019, from https://lonerwolf.com/chakra-balancing/

Introducing Chakra Healing with Anodea Judith. (n.d.). Retrieved November 1, 2019, from https://www.mindvalley.com/chakra/

Visualizing with Color. (2008, January 18). Retrieved November 1, 2019, from https://www.ideafit.com/fitness-library/visualizing-with-color

20 Minute Chakra Balancing, Cleansing, and Healing Meditation and Visualization / Mindful Movement. (2017, June 6). Retrieved November 1, 2019, from https://www.youtube.com/watch?v=x-HT10HErYk&feature=youtu.be

CPSIA information can be obtained
at www.ICGtesting.com
Printed in the USA
LVHW111554011221
704980LV00017B/1064